6-99 ✓

D0231327

CAT

The author

Angela Gair

Angela Gair is an experienced
writer and freelance editor and
has written on many subjects,
including painting and drawing,
gardening and decorating. She is
also a life-long cat-lover and
author of Caring for Your Cat,
published by *HarperCollins* in
association with Cats Protection.
She lives in London with her
three rescue cats, Charlie,
William and Mischa.

ACKNOWLEDGEMENTS

The publishers would like to thank the
following for their kind assistance in
producing this book:
Fiona and Lee Adams, Clare Archer,
Clare Bridges, Lisa Cameron, Sue Clarke,
Rolf Clayton, Karen Cleyer, Gillian
Crossley-Holland, Lindsey Dorrill, Lisa
Feacey, Carole Florey, Deborah Love,
Karen Lynn, Jill Macdonald, Louise
Malone, Mrs Miller, Wendy Raphael,
Rebecca Reeve, Carol Reynolds, Marion
Rutherford, Peggy Schoeberl, Tracy
Stewart and Vivianne Turner.
Our thanks also to David Taylor BVMS,
FRCVS, FZS, for checking the Health section.

DEDICATION
This book is dedicated to the memory
of Mouse, the best little grey cat in
the world.

CAT

ANGELA GAIR

First published in 2000 by
HarperCollins*Publishers*
77-85 Fulham Palace Road
Hammersmith
London W6 8JB

Collins is a registered trademark of
HarperCollins Publishers Limited.

The HarperCollins website address
is www.**fire**and**water**.com

05 04 03 02 01 00
9 8 7 6 5 4 3 2 1

© HarperCollins*Publishers* Ltd 2000

Angela Gair asserts the moral right
to be identified as the author of
this work.

A catalogue record of this book is
available from the British Library.

ISBN 0 00 413401 X

THIS BOOK WAS CREATED BY
SP Creative Design for
HarperCollins*Publishers* **Ltd**
EDITOR: Heather Thomas
DESIGN AND PRODUCTION:
Rolando Ugolini
PHOTOGRAPHY:
Charlie Colmer: pages 1, 3, 4, 5, 6, 10,
11, 12, 13, 14, 15, 16, 17, 18, 19 (top),
22, 25, 26, 27, 28, 29, 30, 32, 33, 34,
35, 40, 41, 45, 46, 47, 48, 51, 52, 53,
54, 55, 56 (top), 57 (top), 60, 63, 64
(left), 65, 69, 73, 76, 83, 85 (bottom),
89, 91, 97, 105, 108, 121, 122
David Dalton: pages 56 (bottom), 58
(bottom), 61, 62, 64 (right), 66, 75,
79, 85 (top), 86 (top), 87, 112, 115
Bruce Tanner: pages 13 (bottom right),
19 (bottom), 31, 37, 38, 39, 42, 44,
49, 57 (bottom), 58 (top), 59, 71, 81,
86 (bottom), 99, 111
Richard Palmer: pages 8, 82, 90, 101

COLOUR REPRODUCTION BY
Colourscan, Singapore
PRINTED AND BOUND BY
Printing Express Ltd, Hong Kong

Contents

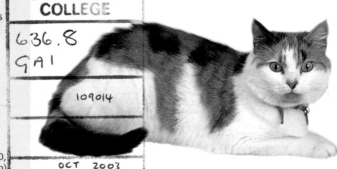

While every reasonable care was taken in the compilation of this
publication, the Publisher and Author cannot accept liability for
any loss, damage, injury or death resulting from the keeping of
cats by user(s) of this publication, or from the use of any materials,
equipment, methods or information recommended in this
publication or from any errors or omissions that may be found in
the text of this publication or that may occur at a future date,
except as expressly provided by law.

PLEASE SHUT
THE GATE

Introduction

It's official. The dog is no longer man's best friend, his place at the fireside having been taken by the cat. Britain now has around eight million pet cats compared to around six million dogs. Cats also outnumber dogs in the United States and in many European countries.

There are many reasons for the recent rise in feline popularity worldwide. Cats are supremely adaptable creatures and fit in very well with today's busy lifestyle. Quiet and self-cleaning, they are easy to look after and more independent than other household pets (you don't have to take a cat on a five-mile hike after a busy day at work). At the same time, we have come to appreciate cats for their therapeutic qualities. They are very loving and affectionate, and when the going gets tough just stroking and playing with a cat has a calming effect. It is hard to feel stressed when watching a cat stretching out luxuriously on the hearth rug and listening to his deep-throated purr.

Felines have an elegance, grace and composure that is quite captivating. Leonardo da Vinci himself dubbed the cat 'Nature's Masterpiece', and it is easy to see why. Lithe, lissom and languid, they make beautiful shapes whether sitting, lying, playing, washing, hunting or sleeping. Having a cat is like having a living sculpture in your home.

Whether you share your life with a lovable moggy or a perfect pedigree, you'll know that there is much more to these fascinating creatures than meets the eye. In the home they are our purring fireside companions, content to curl up by the fire and to be fed and pampered. But on the other side of the cat flap they transform into free-living wild creatures and solitary hunters. Yes, they do have their naughty side — they shred the furniture, dig up the flower beds and indulge in ear-splitting slanging matches in the middle of the night. But any cat-lover will accept these small lapses from grace with a smile and a shrug. For beneath the thin veneer of domestication, cats are wild at heart, with an independent spirit that can never truly be tamed — a quality which has guaranteed them a unique place in human affection.

CHAPTER ONE

The story of the cat

Man's love affair with the cat has lasted some 4,000 years and, like any love affair, it has had its share of ups and downs. At various times the cat has been revered and worshipped, reviled as an instrument of Satan, and cherished as a guardian of hearth and home. As we cross the threshold into the twenty-first century, it looks as if cat and human will live 'happily ever after'.

The domestic cat we know and love is a direct descendant of the African wild cat (*Felis lybica*), an inhabitant of North Africa. This small, elegant feline is thought to have been domesticated by the Ancient Egyptians around 2000BC. It seems that wild cats began approaching human settlements along the banks of the Nile, attracted by the rodents that infested the Egyptians' vast grain stores. By picking off the rats and mice, as well as the poisonous snakes, the cats endeared themselves to the people, and gradually they became part of household life. The Egyptians admired the cat not only for its prowess as a hunter but also for its grace, beauty and

Did you know?

Egyptian families kept cats as a mark of respect to the gods, and when a pet cat died the entire household went into mourning, demonstrating their grief by shaving off their eyebrows.

CHAPTER
ONE

Gentler-natured cats

Tortoiseshell cats are nearly always female. Only one in 200 torties are male, and they are invariably sterile. Because they carry an extra female chromosome they are effectively masculinized females; they are much gentler in nature than the average tom cat!

independent spirit, and in time it achieved the status of sacred feline deity. When a cat died it was mummified and laid to rest in a special burial chamber. The penalty for killing one, even by accident, was death. Of all the domestic animals, only a cat could earn the love and respect of man in return for doing, well, nothing much at all, really!

Although it was forbidden to take cats out of Egypt, some were smuggled out by Phoenician traders and taken to Italy. From there they were introduced to the rest of Europe by the Romans. Eventually, cats were taken to other parts of the globe by traders and settlers as 'ship's cats'. Even today, sailors believe that cats bring good luck to a ship, and, of course, they are useful in dispatching rodents.

Cats in the Middle Ages

While cats continued to lead a charmed existence in other parts of the world during the Middle Ages, their European cousins were not so lucky. Because of its links with paganism, the cat was denounced as evil by the Christian church and for almost 500 years it suffered appalling persecution. Satan's favourite form was believed to be a black cat. Old women living alone

Below: *Pure black cats are now fairly rare due to the efforts of the Christian church in the Middle Ages.*

with their cats were often denounced as witches and their feline companions as their 'familiars' (familiar spirits), and both were drowned or burnt at the stake.

Cats as household pets

It was not until the seventeenth century that cats regained acceptance, but they have not looked back since. By Victorian times they had become pampered household pets, and today it seems that cat-worship is with us once again! During the last century the cat's standard of living has risen dramatically. Where once it was merely tolerated as a useful rat-catcher, the cat is now recognised as a faithful companion and cosseted with the best of food and a warm and cosy home.

Did you know?

Because so many cats were killed during the Middle Ages the rat population in Europe multiplied unchecked. Rat fleas carry bubonic plague ('Black Death') which killed some 25 million people between the fourteenth and seventeenth centuries.

BASIC CAT TYPES

Thanks to generations of domestication and selective breeding, both moggies and purebred cats come in every permutation of type and colour. The main features that vary are coat colour and markings, length and type of coat, and overall body type or conformation.

Cobby type

Typical of the 'cobby' type of cat are the Persian and the Exotic Shorthair. They are short, compact and low on the legs, with broad shoulders and rump, a rounded head shape and a short, thick tail.

❖ *Persian chocolate smoke*

Foreign type

The foreign type is svelte and elegant, with a slim body, long tail and slender legs. They are fine-boned, with a wedge-shaped head, large, pricked ears and slanting eyes. The Siamese, Foreign Shorthair and Egyptian Mau fall into this category.

❖ *Siamese*

▌Muscular type

This is a sturdy cat, with strong
bones and a thick body set on
short but well-proportioned legs.
The head is apple-shaped, and
rounded at the top. It has
well-developed cheeks and
a short, broad
nose. Typical
of this type are
the Burmese
and the British and
American Shorthairs.

❖ *Blue Burmese*

▌Types of eyes

Cats' eyes come in three basic shapes: round, almond and slanted. Cats
with round eyes include the British Shorthair and Persian. Cats with
almond-shaped eyes include the Abyssinian and Tonkinese. The Siamese
and Foreign Shorthair have slanted eyes. Eye colours range from green to
gold, hazel and even vivid blue.

❖ *Round eyes* ❖ *Almond eyes* ❖ *Slanted eyes*

POPULAR CAT BREEDS

Pedigree cats are extremely beautiful animals which combine elegance and grace with lovable traits. There are well over a hundred recognised pedigree breeds of cat today, and new ones are being introduced all the time. Some of the most popular cat breeds are described on the pages that follow.

LONGHAIRED CATS

▌Persian Longhair

■ *Appearance:* With its long, thick, fabulous coat, the Persian is the ultimate 'glamour-puss'. The body is cobby in type, with short, thick legs and a bushy tail, a round head, flat face, and large, round, brilliantly coloured eyes. Persians are bred in a wide range of colours and markings.

■ *Temperament:* Persians are placid, affectionate, and adapt well to indoor life. The colourpoint,

❖ *Persian chocolate smoke*

chocolate and lilac varieties, having some Siamese
blood, are more inquisitive and lively.

■ *Comments:* Don't even consider a Persian unless
you are able and willing to give it
a thorough grooming every
day to prevent the coat
matting. The flat face
can make Persians more
prone to breathing
problems and runny
eyes than other cats.
They are also prone
to develop bladder
stones in later life.

❖ *Red smoke
cameo Persian*

SEMI-LONGHAIRED CATS

Maine Coon

■ *Appearance:* A hardy, thick-coated American breed, large and
powerfully built, with a long body and long, flowing tail. The
head is large and wedge-shaped, the ears pointed and well-
tufted, and the eyes large and expressive. The coat is dense,
lustrous and shaggy and comes in a wide variety of colours and
patterns. The best-known variety is the original brown tabby
form, whose patterning resembles the coat of the racoon.

■ *Temperament:* Loving, companionable and quiet, they make
ideal family pets. Maine Coons are known for the soft little
chirping sounds they make, and for their habit of sleeping in
odd places (possibly a throw-back to their farm-cat ancestry).

■ *Comments:* This breed is not suited to indoor life as it needs
plenty of space in which to explore and let off steam.

CHAPTER
ONE

Birman

■ *Appearance:* The body is long and low and set on short, strong legs. The white paws are its distinguishing feature: the front legs are gloved in white and the back legs are white at the front, with white 'gauntlets' extending up the back. The pale coat appears dusted with gold and the dark points come in a range of colours. The hairs are long and silky, but not prone to matting. The large, round eyes are china blue.

■ *Temperament:* Gentle, tolerant of children and dogs and enjoying good health, Birmans make ideal family pets.

❖ *Blue point Birman*

❖ *Chocolate point Birman*

SHORTHAIRED CATS

▍Siamese

■ *Appearance:* Elegant and aristocratic, with a slender, fine-limbed body and long tail. The head is wedge-shaped with a long, straight nose, large, pointed ears and sapphire blue, slanted eyes. The coat is short, sleek and silky. In the classic seal-point variety the body is cream and the points are seal-brown. Other point colours include blue, chocolate, red, cream, lilac and tortie.

■ *Temperament:* As boisterous as it is beautiful, the Siamese craves human company and will 'converse' with you in its inimitable raucous voice. Highly intelligent, active, inquisitive and extrovert, it can be a very demanding pet, but will reward you with great loyalty, affection and hours of amusement. 'We are Siamese and we DO please...'

■ *Comments:* The Siamese hates to be left by itself; if bored or lonely it can be mischievous and will wail insistently. It is not a breed for busy working people.

▍Did you know?

Siamese kittens are pure white at birth; the dark points on the mask, legs, paws and tail appear as the kittens mature. The points are also temperature-sensitive; kittens reared in a very cold environment become dark all over, while those reared in a very hot environment remain pale all over, with no dark points.

CHAPTER
ONE

▮ British Shorthair

■ *Appearance:* A compact, well-muscled cat with a broad chest and short, sturdy legs with large, round paws. The tail is thick, with a rounded tip. The head is round and broad-cheeked, the eyes round and

wide-set. The plush, dense, easy-care coat comes in a wide range of colours and patterns.

❖ *Chocolate British shorthair*

The American shorthair is descended from the British shorthair. It is rather larger than its British cousin, with a less rounded face and longer legs and tail.

■ *Temperament:* A robust and hardy cat with a calm, easy-going nature, the British Shorthair makes a good pet for children.

❖ *Cream British shorthair*

❖ *Lilac cream British shorthair*

Burmese

■ *Appearance:* The Burmese is descended from a Foreign-type brown female imported into the United States from Burma in the 1930s and cross-bred with a Siamese. It has the lithe and elegant body shape of the Siamese, but slightly smoother and rounder, and a smooth, glossy coat. In addition to the original seal brown colour, there are lilac, blue, platinum, champagne, chocolate, red and cream colours, as well as four tortie varieties. The head is a medium-wedge shape, with high cheekbones. The wide-set eyes are huge, round and golden.

❖ Blue
Burmese

■ *Temperament:* Burmese cats are intelligent, confident and very playful. They are great 'people cats' and love to be involved in family life. They like heights, and delight in observing the world from the tops of cupboards and suchlike.

■ *Comments:* Burmese hate to be left alone all day and can be mischievous if bored. Their friendliness, combined with curiosity and a certain wanderlust, can put them at risk of getting lost or stolen. Appropriate precautions need to be taken.

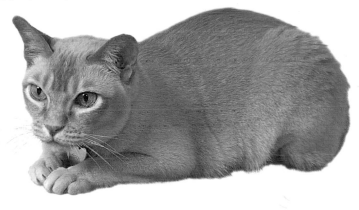

❖ Golden
Burmese

Tonkinese

■ *Appearance:* Originating in Canada, the Tonkinese is the result of crossing a seal-point Siamese with a sable Burmese. Its body is elegant and lithe, yet firm and muscular, resembling that of the Burmese more than the Siamese. The medium-short coat is fine, soft and silky. The eyes are wide and softly almond-shaped, and are a striking aquamarine colour. It comes in a wide range of subtle colours with darker points.

■ *Temperament:* Exceptionally intelligent, lively and inquisitive, 'Tonks' are quite a handful. Bold and friendly, they crave attention and will follow their owner around the house. They love to perch on high places and survey their domain.

■ *Comments:* Beware — the Tonk is not a cat to be ignored. Ideally there should be someone at home all day. If you can handle it, two Tonks will keep each other company.

Exotic Shorthair

■ *Appearance:* This breed originates from America, created by crossing Persians with American Shorthairs. The result is a cat with all the beauty of a Persian, but with a short coat. The Exotic is medium-sized and stocky, with short, sturdy legs and a short tail. The head is broad, with a flat face and short, snub nose. The eyes are large, round and brilliant. The fur is dense, plush and soft, and slightly longer than fur seen on most shorthair cats. It is bred in all colours and patterns, including colourpoint and tabby.

■ *Temperament:* Nicknamed 'the lazy man's Persian', this cat has a similar temperament to the Persian, but without the demands of daily grooming. The Exotic is docile and loving and seldom makes a sound, but is slightly more playful than the Persian and gets on well with children and dogs.

Abyssinian

Did you know?

Abyssinians are often called 'rabbit cats'. This is because their fur resembles that of wild rabbits.

■ *Appearance:* With its lithe, muscular body, large ears and tawny coat, the 'Aby' resembles a small wild cat. Each hair of the dense, soft coat is ticked with three or four colours. The original colour is a ruddy brown ticked with black, and there are many variations including sorrel (red), blue, lilac and chocolate. The almond-shaped eyes are brilliant and expressive and may be amber, hazel or green, with a dark rim.

■ *Temperament:* A lively and intelligent cat that loves to be involved in family life. Like the Siamese, it will investigate things with its paws rather than its nose.

■ *Comments:* Abyssinians are not suited to indoor life as they become restless when kept confined.

Somali

■ *Appearance:* The Somali is a semi-longhaired variant of the Abyssinian, with a ruff, a floating fox-like tail and little tufts of hair between the toes. It comes in over twenty colours. Each hair along its upper body is ticked with six to twelve alternating bands of colour, producing a sparkling shimmer when it moves. Its striking facial markings give it an appealing expression.

❖ *Somali*

■ *Temperament:* Intelligent, affectionate and sweet-natured, the Somali will greet you with a pretty trill.

CHAPTER TWO

Understanding your cat

Even though most cats today live in a safe, domestic environment, they still retain many of the physical and behavioural characteristics of their wild ancestors. An understanding of feline behaviour will help you to develop a stronger and more loving bond with your cat and to keep him healthy and happy.

E volution has shaped the cat into a perfect hunter. Its body is a miracle of physical engineering, designed both for ruthless attack and agile defence. The flexible, almost elastic spine gives the cat a wide range of movement and it can squeeze itself into the smallest of spaces. The supple yet powerful muscles are another aid to speed and agility, enabling the cat to sprint, pounce, climb and jump with the ease and grace of an athlete. As a nocturnal hunter, the cat has acute senses, not only for tracking and catching prey but also to help it to evade predators. Even when dozing, the cat is receptive to sound and able to spring into action at the slightest hint of danger.

Did you know?

Cats were life-savers during the Blitz on Britain in World War II. Their acute hearing enabled them to sense enemy aircraft approaching from afar. As they scurried for cover, their owners followed suit.

Cat senses

All the sense organs of the cat, as a nocturnal hunter, are highly developed. In fact, cats' senses are so acute that they are often reputed to be endowed with supernatural powers. Tales abound of cats predicting earthquakes, tornadoes and other disasters, the most likely explanation being that they are able to pick up sounds and vibrations that humans cannot hear.

Ears

Cats have much more acute hearing than humans and even dogs. There are twenty muscles in each ear, and the ears can rotate independently, enabling the cat to track and pinpoint the precise direction and distance of a sound (they seem particularly attuned to the sound of a can-opener being operated...).

Eyes

Contrary to popular belief, cats cannot see in the dark, but they can see better in poor light than humans. Their eyes are large and sit well forward on the head, giving a wide angle of vision. The pupils react instantly to changing light conditions, contracting to narrow slits in bright light and dilating to full circles in dim light. A layer of special cells lies behind the retina which act as a mirror; when the pupils are wide open, in the dark, light reflects back off these cells. This is why cats' eyes appear to shine in the dark.

Nose

The cat's sense of smell is fourteen times more sensitive than a human's. This explains why cats are not fooled when we try to disguise their medicines in their food!

Did you know?

White cats can be blue-eyed, orange-eyed or odd-eyed (having one blue and one orange eye). Sadly, those with blue eyes are almost always born deaf. Odd-eyed cats are occasionally deaf on the side of the blue eye. Orange-eyed white cats have no hearing problems.

Below: *The domestic cat shares many characteristics with its wild counterparts.*

Tongue

The surface of the cat's tongue is covered in tiny abrasive papillae which enable it to rasp meat from bones and to remove loose hairs during grooming. The tongue can also be curled in from the sides to form a 'spoon' for lapping up liquids.

Teeth

The cat has a set of thirty teeth, designed for eating meat. There are four large canines which hold and kill prey, twelve incisors for gnawing and fourteen back teeth which act like scissors, shearing meat into small pieces.

Whiskers

Cats have about twelve whiskers below the nose on each side of the face, with additional ones above the eyes. The whiskers have nerves at their base and can detect even the slightest touch.

The righting reflex

Cats are able to walk nimbly along narrow branches, fences and roof tops because the balancing mechanism in their ears is highly tuned. If a cat does fall from a height, it will often (though not always) land safely on all four paws, thanks to the 'righting reflex'. The fluid-filled cavities within the ear transmit information to the brain on the position of the cat's head relative to gravity and the cat rotates its body so as to land the right way up.

Tail

The tail is in fact an extension of the spine. It is used as a steering and balancing mechanism when climbing and jumping. The tail is also an important means of communication: held high, it is a sign of greeting; flicked from side to side, it is a sign of anger or aggression.

Below: *Approaching with tail erect, this cat shows his friendly intentions.*

Claws

A cat's claws are important tools needed in fighting with rivals, catching prey and climbing trees. Cats keep their claws in trim by stropping them on tree trunks and fence posts to pull off the old outer layer of claw and expose the new one beneath.

Coat

Cats can tolerate extremes of temperature because their fur acts as a very efficient insulator. The guard hairs on the coat contain highly sensitive touch receptors. A cat on the defensive fluffs up his coat and his tail fur in an attempt to appear bigger.

The Jacobson's organ

Cats, in common with lions, tigers and horses, have an extra sense organ which humans lack. Known as Jacobson's organ, it is situated in the roof of the mouth and allows the cat literally to 'taste' smells. The cat curls its lips back (a behaviour known as 'flehmen') to allow scents, left by other cats, to enter the mouth and travel up through two openings behind the front teeth into a tiny chamber, where they are concentrated and absorbed.

Did you know?

The Ancient Egyptian word for cat was 'mau', which meant 'to see'. The Egyptians believed that the cat's luminescent eyes mirrored the rays of the sun and protected mankind from darkness.

Right: *Tabbies are the basic 'wild' form from which all other feline coat colours and types have evolved.*

Instincts and behaviour

When you share your life with a cat, it is sometimes easy to forget that he is not just a four-legged, fur-covered member of your own family. As a species, however, cats have their own complex system of behaviour, which relates directly to their wild origins and has remained strong despite thousands of years of domestication. Their hunting instinct and territorial behaviour, for example, are still very much in evidence.

Grooming

For an animal that hates water, cats certainly spend a lot of time washing themselves! Thorough grooming by licking the coat with the tongue serves many functions: it removes loose hairs and smooths down the fur so that it insulates the body more

Right: *Cats are fastidious creatures and spend many of their waking hours washing and grooming.*

efficiently; it stimulates the glands at the base of the hairs which waterproof the coat; in hot weather, licking spreads saliva which cools the cat as it evaporates; it also spreads sebum across the coat, and when this is exposed to sunlight it produces vitamin D, which is ingested by the cat.

The catnip response

If you have a garden, give your cat a treat and plant a patch of catmint in a sunny spot. *Nepeta cataria*, also known as catnip, is a an attractive plant which produces blue flowers in summer. Oils in the leaves contain a chemical component that sends cats into a state of bliss. They sniff the plant and then roll on it, releasing the aroma. You can also buy packets of dried catnip leaves and toys impregnated with catnip.

Purring

How, and why, cats purr is something of a mystery, even to the experts who study these things. It is thought that the cat has additional membranes close to the vocal cords and purring results from their vibration, but this has not been proved. The purr signals pleasure, contentment and affection. Sometimes it is a not very subtle form of begging for food! Mother cats purr when giving birth and suckling their kittens. The vibrations act as a homing device for the kittens, who are born blind, virtually deaf and with no sense of smell. Strangely, ill or injured cats also purr, perhaps to comfort themselves. Cats also purr a lot when they are incubating cat flu.

Sleeping

There are many ailments that can afflict a cat, but insomnia is definitely not one of them! Cats spend up to two-thirds of their day sleeping, albeit in short 'catnaps'.

Right: *Mother Nature spends millions of years perfecting the supreme hunter, only to find her creation lolling on the hearthrug wearing a 'peel me a prawn' expression!*

Right: *When a cat or a kitten plays, he is practising his hunting skills.*

In the wild, it is their way of conserving energy for the intense activities of hunting food and defending territory. The pampered house cat may not do much hunting, but he gets in plenty of shut-eye anyway!

Hunting

Often those who love cats also love birds and small mammals and find it hard to accept that their sweet little cat can be a ruthless killer. Even the best-fed cat will not pass up the chance to hunt mice and birds; it is a deep-rooted instinct, and when real prey is not available a cat will divert his natural instincts onto substitute 'prey', such as a toy or a dangled piece of string.

It is movement, not hunger, that triggers a cat's hunting instinct. Alerted by the tiniest movement in the grass, the cat stalks his victim, slinking low to the ground with eyes fixed and ears alert. When he is within striking range, he crouches behind cover and treads with his hind legs, then pounces on his prey. Now the cat's instinct is to preserve himself from injury; a bite from a rat could prove lethal. So he bites at the head of the victim or tosses it in the air to disorientate it. If the victim tries to escape, the movement triggers the hunting response again. To us, the cat

Did you know?

Towser, a female tortoiseshell cat, was 'employed' as a rodent-catcher by a whisky distillery in Scotland until her death in 1987. During her working life she notched up a tally of nearly 29,000 mice, averaging at least three kills a day.

appears to be cruelly 'torturing' his prey, releasing and
recapturing it several times before finally delivering the death-
bite. In fact, this is a sign of an inept hunter. Hunting is an
instinct, but bringing the hunt to a swift and successful
conclusion (the nape bite, designed to sever the spinal cord and

Above: *This cat is stropping his claws on a tree, at the same
time leaving a scent message for other cats.*

Above: *Even a neutered male cat will mark out his own territory and then fiercely defend his 'patch' against other feline intruders.*

bring instant death) is a skill that must be learned. Cats raised by non-hunting mothers often do not master this skill, and once they have caught their prey they seem unsure what to do with it.

Territorial instinct

The domesticated cat has no need to hunt or to defend his territory against competitors in order to survive, but the instinct to do so is still there. All cats establish distinct territories for themselves, centred on their home base. Territory size varies according to the number of cats in the area and the space available, and entire toms have much larger territories than females and neutered males. If a male wanders into another male's territory a fight may ensue, but cats prefer to behave in a civilized manner and they will adopt recognised routes between territories so as to avoid conflict.

Scent marking

One of the most important ways in which cats communicate with each other is by scent. Cats scent-mark to define the boundaries of their territory and to attract members of the opposite sex. The most common way of marking, particularly in entire toms, is by spraying pungent urine. Whereas a cat squats to urinate, spraying is performed from a standing position. The cat backs up to a vertical object and aims a few short spurts of urine backwards at his target with his tail raised and quivering and back slightly arched.

Other territorial markers include rubbing against objects with the head and body to deposit scents produced by sebaceous glands in the skin, and by scratching posts or tree trunks to deposit scent secretions from glands on the paw pads.

Above: *Cats often use fences and gateposts as vantage points from which to keep an eye on their territory. This cat is marking out his territory by rubbing his sebaceous cheeks against the post.*

The mating game

Cats are promiscuous creatures. From the age of about six months onwards, females come into 'heat' (oestrus) at frequent intervals during the spring and summer. Each heat lasts three to six days. The female, or 'queen', indicates her readiness to mate by rolling around on the ground, rubbing incessantly against objects and calling loudly to attract a tom. If stroked, she will crouch and raise her tail.

When the female is ready to accept her mate, she will flirt with him, roll provocatively and then raise her rear and hold her tail to one side. The tom grips her by the nape with his teeth and mounts her. The sex act, which lasts only a few seconds, triggers ovulation. As the tom withdraws, the queen emits a loud cry and lashes out at him. The tom beats a hasty retreat and watches her from a safe distance while she goes into a display of rolling, rubbing and voluptuous stretching. Both cats then groom themselves before engaging in a repeat performance.

The queen may mate several more times during oestrus, and not necessarily always with the same tom.

Did you know?

An unneutered female cat is called a queen — but not because of her royal bearing. It comes from the old word 'quean', meaning a hussy. If you've ever witnessed the wanton behaviour of a female cat in heat, this makes sense!

CHAPTER
TWO

The happy event

The queen carries her kittens for approximately sixty-three days. When the birth is imminent she searches for a dark, secluded place to make her nest. Even with her first litter, a queen knows instinctively what to do and will purr throughout the entire delivery. The first kitten is born about fifteen minutes after the onset of labour. Immediately the mother licks her newborn to remove the birth sac and to stimulate its breathing. She then chews off the umbilical cord and eats the placenta. She does this to remove it from predators which might be attracted to it and harm the newborn kittens, and also because the placenta provides her with essential nutrients in the days after giving birth, when she is unable to hunt. Most queens give birth to between three and six kittens (the average is four) and the interval between births varies from five to sixty minutes.

Bringing up baby

Cats make excellent mothers, feeding, grooming and protecting their kittens when they are young and then teaching them the skills they will need to survive in adulthood. In feral colonies, the females often share in the care of each other's young.

Did you know?

An Italian legend says that at the moment Mary gave birth to Jesus, a female cat living in the same manger had a litter of kittens. Leonardo da Vinci included a cat and kittens in many of his studies of the Madonna and Child.

The first few days

Kittens are born with their eyelids closed and their ears folded back, so they are blind and deaf. An inborn rooting reflex helps them to locate their mother's teats. The first milk, secreted during the first few days after birth, is called the colostrum. It is packed with nutrients and antibodies which protect the kittens against disease for the first twelve weeks of life. While

Above: *At the milk bar! A mother cat's milk provides her kittens with all the essential nutrients needed for healthy development.*

feeding, the kittens use their front paws to 'knead' the mother's belly to stimulate the flow of milk (a behaviour which often extends into adulthood, when a cat sits on his owner's lap, purring contentedly and kneading with his front paws. This gives the owner pleasure mixed with pain, since the cat's claws are usually extended!)

The first week
During this time the kittens do nothing but suckle and sleep. Deaf, blind and unable to walk, they are totally dependent on

CHAPTER
TWO

Above: *Now, don't forget to wash behind your ears! The grooming instinct is inborn in cats, and is seen in kittens as young as three weeks old.*

their mother for survival. She licks and nuzzles them to encourage them to feed, and stimulates them to eliminate their wastes by licking their behinds and then cleans them up.

The second week
By now the kittens are growing rapidly and they can propel themselves by crawling. Their eyes, which are always blue at this stage, start to open. The ear flaps begin to unfold and stand upright and the kittens are able to hear clearly now. They may try to stand and take their first wobbly steps.

The third week
The milk teeth start to break through. The kittens are now eager to explore their surroundings and start to play with objects and with each other. At this stage the mother still spends most of her time with her kittens, but she starts to prepare them for their independence by leaving them on their own for short periods.

In the wild, she kills prey animals and brings them back to the nest to eat in front of them.

The fourth and fifth weeks
By the end of the fourth week the kittens are able to toilet without their mother's help. In a domestic situation they learn how to use a litter tray by copying their mother.

The sixth week
The wild mother starts to wean her young onto solid food by restricting their access to her milk and bringing back injured prey for them to practise their

Did you know?
Some of the world's most notorious dictators — Alexander the Great, Napoleon, Hitler — hated and feared cats. Obviously they sensed that this is a creature that refuses to be conquered, enslaved or possessed by anyone!

Below: *Kittens spend most of their time sleeping because they use up so much energy in play.*

Left: *Kittens love to play – with each other and with humans and toys. They will jump up and 'bat' at objects held above them.*

hunting skills on. This is essential for her survival, as feeding her brood as well as using energy on hunting saps her strength.

The seventh week

The kittens are sleeping less and spending much of their time engaged in mock-fights with their siblings. Their spats may look cute and comical to us, but they are in fact honing their senses and reactions and learning the hunting routines of stalking, pouncing and capturing.

Eight weeks onwards

By the time they reach eight weeks old the kittens are fully weaned, and by twelve weeks they are fully independent of their mother. Between three and six months old the milk teeth are shed

Right: *Kittens experience a dramatic rate of growth during the first few months of life.*

Above: *Kittens are naturally inquisitive and enjoy playing together and practising their hunting skills.*

and replaced by a set of permanent adult teeth. In the wild, the female young often stay with their mothers until they themselves become mothers. The males leave the family group and go off in search of territory of their own.

Socialization

If a domestic kitten is not used to being handled by humans from an early age it may grow up fearful and hostile. There is an important period, between the ages of four and seven weeks, when kittens should be handled and played with by a variety of adults and children several times a day and exposed to other pets, everyday domestic noises and so on. This socialization period is crucial if the kitten is to grow up to be a friendly, outgoing and playful adult.

CHAPTER THREE

Acquiring a cat

Cats are known for their independence, but the fact is that the cat or kitten you adopt will rely on you to care for him throughout his life — and that can be as long as twenty years or more. Remember, a little careful thought before you acquire a cat will help you to avoid making an impulsive decision which you may later regret.

Lots of owners say they did not actually choose their cat, he just walked in! Nevertheless, the decision to own (or be owned by) a cat should not be taken lightly. There are many important things to consider. Try to answer the questions below as honestly as possible; they will help you decide if you really are ready to share your home with a feline.

■ Are your home and garden safe for a cat?

■ Do you live near a busy road?

■ Who will look after your cat when you are away from home?

■ Are you sure that no one in your family is allergic to cats?

■ How much can you afford? You will have to take into account: food, cat litter, parasite

Did you know?

The USA's 'first cat' — President Clinton's black and white cat Socks — was originally found as a stray. He now lives in the lap of luxury and receives several sacks of fan mail a day!

CHAPTER
THREE

Right: *What's theirs is theirs and what's yours is theirs too! Cats are no respecters of your personal space, so expect hairs on your bed and paw prints on your furniture.*

control, neutering, vaccinations and annual boosters, veterinary costs if your cat is ill or injured and possible boarding costs for your cat during your holidays

■ Are you houseproud? Can you cope if your cat scratches your furniture and leaves hairs and muddy paw prints everywhere?

■ If you intend having children in the future, are you certain you will want to keep the cat on?

Above: *The combination of cats' claws and antique furniture may be an uncomfortable one for some, but this cat seems to have got away with it!*

Choosing a cat

Having decided that you definitely have the time and also the committment to give a cat, you need to identify the right kind of feline for you and your family.

Cat or kitten?

Kittens are adorable and bags of fun, and you will get a great deal of pleasure from nurturing a little one and watching him grow up. But will a kitten fit in with your lifestyle? Do you have the time and energy to cope with a supercharged funpack running up the curtains and demolishing your delicate houseplants? Is your home unoccupied for most of the day? Remember that a young kitten needs lots of attention and will become bored and lonely on his own. He may get into mischief or hurt himself. Also, he needs to be fed several times a day. Do you have children? While older children and kittens can be best friends, young children will need

Right: *If you are looking for an affectionate, amusing and intelligent companion, then a cat is the pet for you.*

constant supervision; the combination of boisterous youngster and tiny kitten can be a recipe for disaster!

An adult cat is the better choice for you if you are out at work all day. Older cats are more placid and affectionate than kittens, and as long as you make the time to play with your cat, he will remain active and kittenish well into old age. You will still need to teach your children respect for animals (a cat will defend itself with teeth and claws in response to squeezing or tail-pulling) but an adult cat knows better than a kitten how to keep out of harm's way.

Right: *Only get a kitten if you are at home and have the time to play with him.*

Male or female?

With regard to temperament and behaviour, there is nothing to choose between a male and a female cat as long as they are neutered. Both sexes make equally good, affectionate pets.

Pedigree or moggy?

By far the greatest number of domestic cats fall into the category affectionately known as 'moggy'. Moggies come in all colours and coat types, and what they lack in aristocratic breeding they make up for in charm. They also tend to be a little more hardy and longer-lived than their pedigree cousins.

Pedigree cats are, of course, extremely beautiful creatures. Each breed has a distinct temperament and personality, which means you can choose one that fits in with your lifestyle. Siamese cats, for example, are lively and sociable and therefore not a good choice of pet for the busy working person. Persians, on the other hand, are more placid and will adapt well to an indoor lifestyle (but do bear in mind that their long coats need regular grooming). Birmans and Ragdolls are also placid, and good with children. Before making a choice, read up about the different breeds (the most popular breeds are described in Chapter 1) and visit cat shows and talk to breeders.

Below: *The Persian is a good choice of pet if you go out to work. They are very happy to see you when you get home, but they are quite content to sleep during the day.*

Did you know?

The term 'moggy' is believed by some to be a corruption of margay, a small jungle cat of South America. Others attribute the origin of the name to an English music-hall artiste of the 1890s named Moggie Dowser, who wore a wrap around her neck that looked like cat fur.

One cat or two?

The image of the independent, self-sufficient cat can be very misleading. In fact, cats love company, and solitary cats left 'home alone' all day can become unhappy and introverted. If you are out all day, but still feel you would like a cat, why not consider adopting two? A feline that has a companion will be happier and less lonely in your absence, and tends to be more playful and active than a single cat. Of course, two cats will involve twice the cost and twice the responsibility. If this is not an option, it would be fairer to adopt a less demanding pet instead.

Finding a cat

If you have decided on a pedigree cat, the best place to obtain one is from a recognised breeder. These can be contacted through individual cat breed clubs, pet

Below: *Two kittens brought up together will form a strong and lasting bond.*

Above: *Many people acquire their first cat by starting to feed a stray that turns up on the doorstep and eventually worms his way into their affections, and their home.*

magazines, or by visiting cat shows. Owners and breeders will be happy to discuss the finer points of the various breeds to help you decide which one is right for you. When buying a kitten you should be able to see the mother and litter-mates and check that they are healthy and well cared for. A reputable breeder will agree to let your own vet examine the cat before you complete the purchase. A pedigree kitten should be no less than twelve weeks old before it leaves the breeder, and it should be fully inoculated.

Rescue cats

There is never a shortage of unwanted cats and kittens looking for good homes, and the rewards of taking on a neglected pet and seeing it thrive are enormous. Contact rescue organisations in your area; some of them deal specifically with cats. Their

CHAPTER
THREE

volunteer carers are anxious to team up the right pet with the right home, so don't be offended if you are asked a lot of questions about your circumstances before you can adopt an animal. If you have children or dogs, for example, it would be unwise to take on a rescue cat that has had bad experiences with these in the past. The cat's history may be unknown, but the volunteers will know his temperament, and he will have had a veterinary health check and have been neutered if he was old enough.

Other sources

Nowadays, reputable pet shops do not sell kittens. Pet shop kittens are likely to have been taken away from their mother too early and may have both health and behavioural problems as a result. It is very easy to take pity on a helpless kitten, but a sickly one could cost you dear, both emotionally and financially. You are better off getting a cat or kitten from a kind and loving

What to look for

■ A kitten should be at least eight weeks old before it leaves its mother (twelve weeks for a pure-bred kitten). By this age he will be weaned and probably house-trained.

■ Check that the cat's environment is clean and that he is in good health. The eyes, ears and nose should be free from discharge. The mouth and gums should be pink and healthy and the breath sweet. The coat should be soft and smooth, with no sign of fleas.

■ Choose a cat or kitten that is playful and inquisitive and willing to be handled. Avoid one that is nervous and hides in a corner unless you know you have the dedication necessary to 'rehabilitate' it.

Above: *Contrary to popular wisdom, cats and dogs can live together peacably and even develop friendships ... eventually!*

private home. He is more likely to be healthy, and if he is used to being handled by people will be affectionate and playful, and may even be house-trained.

Collecting your cat

Before going to collect your new cat or kitten, make sure you have all the necessary equipment ready, including an appropriate carrying box (see page 56). Smell is very important to cats, so place an old towel or sweater inside the carrier; this will give him a chance to 'sniff out' your home in advance. Discuss the cat's previous diet with the owner so you can continue giving him this for the first few days he is with you, to avoid stomach upsets. Arrange to collect your cat when you can be at home for a few days, to keep him company and help him settle in.

CHAPTER FOUR

Looking after your cat

If you take the trouble to look after your cat, he will reward you with many years of companionship, affection and amusement. In this chapter you will find all the information you need to help keep your cat healthy, happy and fit.

When you bring your new cat or kitten home for the first time, he may be a little nervous. It is best to keep him in one room until he has settled down. Offer him some food and show him his litter tray and bed. It is best for the first few days to give the food he was used to eating in his previous home. Then gradually introduce the food you want to serve over the next few days.

It's only natural for everyone to make a fuss of the new arrival, but remember that cats also like to be left alone sometimes. After a day or two he can be allowed to explore the rest of the house, but ensure that doors and windows leading outside are closed, and block off any fireplaces too; timid cats have been known to bolt up the chimney!

CHAPTER
FOUR

A new cat should be kept indoors for at a week or two, and the same goes for when you move house with your cat. If he is let out too soon and wanders off he may not be able to find his way home. Stay with him on his first few forays into the garden, and let him out before mealtimes rather than after, so that he is encouraged to come home to eat.

▌Registering with a veterinary surgeon

It is wise to arrange a veterinary check-up for your cat as soon as you bring him home. Ask local cat-lovers to recommend one who has a good knowledge of cats and offers a twenty-four hour emergency service. The vet can also advise you about essential things like feeding, vaccination, worming and neutering. If you adopt a stray cat, or a cat from a rescue home, you should always have him health-checked before introducing him to other cats in your household. He may appear healthy but he could be in the incubating stages of an infectious disease. He could even be a 'healthy carrier', i.e. it is possible for a cat to carry a life-threatening disease, such as Feline infectious peritonitis (FIP), and infect other cats without himself showing any symptoms (see page 102). As a precaution, ask your vet to carry out a blood test on the new cat to check for viral infections.

Health insurance

It is worth considering taking out health insurance to cover the cost of veterinary fees. If your cat is taken ill unexpectedly or has an accident, you will have enough to think about without the added worry of large veterinary bills. For a monthly premium costing around the price of a takeaway pizza, pet insurance will cover most of the vet's fees for any course of treatment (except routine treatments such as vaccination and neutering). Some policies also pay out a lump sum if a cat is killed in an accident, lost or stolen. It is recommended that you gather information from several insurance companies, compare their costs and benefits and scrutinise the small print before you take out a policy.

Right: *Regular veterinary check-ups will ensure that your cat stays healthy.*

CHAPTER
FOUR

EQUIPMENT

Below you will find a list of all the
'kit' your cat needs. Some of these
items are essential, some are
optional, and some can be improvised
from household odds and ends.

Carrying basket

❖ *Encased plastic carrier*

A carrying basket is essential for those
trips to the veterinary surgery. A good-quality basket should last
a lifetime. Look for one that is secure, well-ventilated and easy to
clean. There are various designs to choose from.

■ Plastic carriers with a mesh door at the front make a cat feel
secure while allowing him to see out, but persuading a wriggling
bundle of fur to enter through the door
is not always easy. Some models come
apart for easy storage, and the base
section can be used as a cat bed.

■ Baskets made of plastic-coated wire
are a favourite with vets because the
top-opening lid
offers easy access
to the patient.

Left: *A basket
made of metal
coated with plastic will
last for many years and
is easily cleaned.*

❖ Cardboard carrier

❖ *Side opening wire basket*

■ Wicker baskets may look pretty but they are difficult to clean and disinfect.
■ Cardboard carriers are not recommended except for small kittens. A frightened cat may panic and tear his way out. And if he urinates, the cardboard will simply disintegrate.

❖ *Wicker basket*

Feeding bowls

Food and water bowls come in sturdy metal and ceramic and colourful plastic, or you can simply recycle your old crockery. As to shape, cats prefer wide and shallow to small and deep, so that their whiskers don't get in the way when they are eating.

Automatic food dispensers with a timer switch ensure that your cat does not go hungry if you are late home from work.

Right: *Feeding bowls should be placed in a quiet corner of the kitchen, well away from the litter tray.*

Toilet training

Most kittens learn to use a litter tray by copying their mother. Some, however, may need a little help. Kittens often need to use the tray after a meal, so gently lift your kitten on to the tray after feeding, or if you see him sniffing, scratching or crouching in a corner.

Litter tray

Indoor cats, and those kept in at night, will need a litter tray. Choose one that is deep enough to keep your cat from scattering litter when he digs, and large enough to allow him to make a complete turn. Some cats appreciate a little privacy, and a hooded litter tray with a carbon filter will help minimize both unpleasant odours and litter-spill. There are also disposable litter trays, and self-cleaning electronic ones.

Above: *The small litter tray on the left is suitable for a kitten. Adult cats require a large, deep tray (right). Use a plastic scoop to remove soiled litter.*

Litter

Litter comes in various materials, from clay granules to compressed pellets made from recycled wood or paper. The best ones form solid clumps when wet. These are easily removed with a scoop, leaving the rest of the litter fresh and dry. If your cat has come to you from another home, find out what type of litter he used there. Some cats will refuse to use a litter they don't like. Fill the tray to a depth of at least 5–8 cm (2–3 in) and place it in an easily accessible but secluded place, well away from the cat's feeding area.

Remove soiled litter regularly and, once a week, empty the tray completely and wash it with hot water and detergent. Avoid using disinfectants as some are toxic to cats and their smell is repellent to them. Pregnant women should never handle soiled cat litter due to the risk of toxoplasmosis (see page 102).

Never leave a cat indoors without a litter tray. If the cat has to hold its urine for long periods, bacteria will breed in stale urine retained in the bladder and this can cause cystitis.

Cat flap

A cat flap, fitted into the door leading to the back garden, allows your cat the freedom to come and go as he pleases. Most have four settings: in only, out only, locked, and unlocked. Some models are activated by a small magnet or key hung on the cat's collar. These

Did you know?

Sir Isaac Newton is credited with the invention of the cat flap. He is said to have cut two holes in his door: one for his cat and another, smaller one, for her kittens.

Right: *Most cats quickly learn how to use a cat flap, and enjoy the freedom it provides.*

allow only your cat to pass, keeping out unwanted feline visitors. The only disadvantage is that if the key or magnet is lost, your cat won't be able to get in.

Beds and bedding

Cats will sleep anywhere, so a bed is not strictly necessary. A closed cardboard box with a hole cut in one side and lined with soft bedding is perfectly adequate and can be discarded when soiled. If this isn't good enough for darling Fluffy, pet stores sell all manner of snuggly beds and blankets for cats. However, having bought an expensive bed, you may well find that your cat prefers to sleep in the laundry basket or on your favourite sweater!

Scratching post

Cats need to scratch on rough surfaces, to trim their claws and to deposit their scent. Indoor cats tend to use furniture, carpets and wallpaper for this purpose, and even cats with access to trees often scratch indoors, too, possibly to make them feel secure in their 'den'. Ideally, you should train your cat to use a scratching post from an early age; older cats are sometimes more resistant. Pet stores offer a variety of sisal-covered scratching posts, or you can construct one from a tall, bark-covered log attached to a sturdy base. Make sure the post is tall enough to allow your cat a full stretch and

Left: *Snug as a bug. This inviting bed is an ideal shape for a cat to curl up in and feel warm and secure.*

Right: *A scratching post will help to keep your cat's claws in trim — and your furniture intact!*

strong enough so he can really pull on it; he won't use it if it's too short or at all wobbly.

Collar

There are mixed views about using collars as some cats have been strangled when their collar has snagged on a tree branch. Sometimes a cat gets a front leg tangled in his collar and as he struggles free the collar cuts into the skin, causing deep wounds. If your cat needs to wear an identity collar, make sure it includes an elasticated section that will stretch enough to slip over his head if it becomes snagged on a branch. Even better are collars with a breakaway section that snaps open if the collar is pulled hard, allowing the cat to escape. There are also fluorescent collars, designed to be visible to motorists at night.

Bird-lovers will be pleased to know that a special cat collar is now available, designed to protect birds

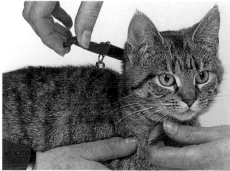

Right: *Fit the collar so that you can easily slip two fingers underneath it. This way it will not choke the cat but is tight enough not to slip off.*

without interfering with cats' natural hunting instincts. As the cat launches itself at a bird, a one-second audio-visual alarm on the collar is triggered, allowing the bird to escape. The noise of the alarm is threatening to birds, but inoffensive to humans and cats.

Grooming aids

For grooming a shorthaired cat you will need a fine-toothed metal comb and perhaps a soft bush. For a longhaired cat you will need a stiff-bristle brush, a wide-toothed comb and possibly a pair of blunt-ended scissors for cutting out knots in the fur.

Grooming equipment

A selection of grooming aids for longhaired and shorthaired cats. Not all of these are essential; for shorthaired cats all you need is a metal comb. Clockwise, from top left: rubber brush; bristle brush; slicker brush; blunt-ended scissors for cutting out knots and tangles; fine-toothed metal combs or flea combs; wide-toothed metal comb.

THE WELL-GROOMED CAT

Grooming should be a regular part of your cat's routine.
Most cats enjoy it, and grooming has several benefits.
It stimulates the circulation, improves muscle
tone and helps to minimize hairballs in the
stomach by removing loose hairs. It also
gives you the opportunity to check for
fleas, ticks and ear mites as well as fight
wounds and abscesses. Grooming is
also a pleasurable bonding experience
between a cat and his owner.

■ Shorthaired cats benefit from
a weekly grooming with a fine-
toothed metal comb and a
natural-bristle or rubber brush
to remove any dead hairs.

■ Semi-longhairs and
plush-coated breeds should
be groomed every few days.

■ Persians have long, fine hair and must
be thoroughly combed and brushed for at least fifteen minutes
daily, otherwise knots and mats quickly form which pull on the
skin and cause great discomfort.

A fur-lined nest

When grooming a longhaired cat in spring, don't throw away
the fur but put it out in the garden in small piles for the birds
to collect and use in their nests. Let your cat do the birds a
favour for a change!

▌ Grooming your cat

Use a comb with long, widely spaced teeth that go deep into the
coat. Comb with the natural lie of the fur, then use a natural
bristle brush to sweep up the coat in the direction of the head.
Any knots should be gently teased out with the fingers. If
necessary, cut them off carefully with blunt-ended scissors.
Sprinkling the coat of longhairs with unperfumed baby powder
once a week will keep it free of grease and more manageable.

If your cat dislikes being groomed, try holding a tasty treat
under his nose and stroking with the other hand. Talk to him to
reassure him, then introduce the comb and gently groom him, a
little at a time, while he is interested in the food. He will soon get

Left: *You can groom and massage
your cat at the same time using a
flexible rubber brush with pointed 'fingers'
that reach through the coat to the
underlying skin.*

Below: *To remove tangles, powder them
with unperfumed talcum powder, then
gently tease them apart with the fingers.*

used to the process and begin to enjoy it. If all else fails, try stroking him while wearing rubber gloves; this will remove the dead hairs without causing him too much alarm.

Bathing a cat
Unless he is a show cat, your pet will need to be bathed only when his coat is very dirty or contaminated with oil. Use just a little warm water and a safe cat shampoo or baby shampoo and rinse well. Wrap the cat in a heated towel and gently rub him. Keep him in a warm room until his coat is completely dry.

Right: *Regular grooming will keep your cat looking his best.*

Claw care

An outdoor cat's claws don't need to be trimmed, but the claws of indoor and elderly cats may need trimming every few weeks. If they become too long they may grow inwards into their pads, causing pain and infection. Your vet can show you how to do this. Press the cat's paw between your finger and thumb to unsheath the claw. Using cat-claw clippers or human nail clippers, snip off just the transparent tip of the claw, avoiding the quick (the part of the claw containing blood vessels and nerves; if you hold the claw against a strong light this is visible as a red line).

CHAPTER
FOUR

Identification

If a lost or injured cat is found, he will have a much better chance of being reunited with his family if he has some means of identification. Various options are available to you.

Collars

A collar bearing an engraved disc or a barrel which holds the owner's name, address and phone number shows that the cat is not a stray but is owned by somebody. A quick-release safety collar is recommended, but if the collar does come off, the cat has lost his means of identification.

Tattoos

In some countries a tattoo inside the ear is the preferred means of identification, but it is rarely used in the UK. A tattoo is easily visible, cannot be lost, and is completely safe.

Microchipping

This method is reliable and permanent method. A vet implants a tiny microchip under the skin at the back of the cat's neck. The chip bears a unique registration code which is registered with the owner's details on a centralized database. If a cat is handed in to a veterinary surgery or animal shelter, it can be scanned to reveal its ID code. Your details will come up on the computer and you will be contacted and reunited with your pet (if you move house, update your details on the database). The disadvantages of microchipping are that it cannot be seen by the naked eye and it is fairly expensive.

Left: *Microchipping is a safe, painless and permanent method of identification for cats.*

PREVENTATIVE CARE

Most vets will tell any pet owner that 'prevention is better than cure'. To ensure a long and healthy life for your cat, the following areas of veterinary health care should be attended to regularly.

▌Vaccination

As the number of pet cats (and strays) rises, the feline world is becoming increasingly crowded. Your cat is bound to come into contact with other cats on his forays outdoors and is at risk of exposure to potentially life-threatening infectious diseases. Even indoor cats are not completely safe as certain viruses can be carried in from outdoors on shoes and clothing. It is therefore essential to have your cat vaccinated against the 'big three' viral diseases: cat flu, Feline enteritis and Feline leukaemia (plus, in some countries, rabies). At present there is no vaccine against Feline immunodeficiency virus in the UK.

For kittens, the primary-vaccination course consists of two injections, one at nine weeks old and the second at twelve weeks. If you adopt a stray or a cat from a rescue centre, wait two weeks before having him vaccinated; if he is incubating the flu virus the vaccine could harm him. Immunity does not take full effect until two weeks after the second injection, so keep your cat indoors until that time. Vaccination cannot protect against a disease once it has taken hold.

To maintain levels of immunity, a booster dose is required every twelve to eighteen months. Some cats may feel a little unwell after vaccination, but unless the symptoms persist for more than two days there is no need to worry. In recent years it has come to light that a tiny percentage of cats have become very ill after receiving booster shots, or developed malignant tumours at the injection-site. This problem is mainly associated with rabies and leukaemia vaccines (in the UK, cats are not vaccinated against rabies). Some vets in the United States now recommend that boosters be given only once every three years after the initial one-year booster, thus reducing the risk of adverse reactions. However, this is open to debate and the risk of a cat catching Feline leukaemia is much greater than the very small risk of vaccine-site tumours. For your own peace of mind you should discuss the pros and cons with your own vet.

You will be given a certificate, which should be updated when the annual booster injections are done. Keep it safe, as you will need it if you ever have to board your cat in a cattery.

Neutering

The issue of stray and unwanted pets continues to be a growing problem. Unless you breed pedigree cats professionally, the kind and responsible thing to do is to have your pet neutered. A cat can be neutered at virtually any age, but ideally it should be done before puberty, at five or six months old. The operation is simple, painless and safe. In a female, 'spaying' consists of removing the womb and the ovaries. For a male, castration consists of removing the testicles.

Did you know?

An unspayed female cat can have up to three litters each year, with up to six kittens in each litter. In five years she could be responsible for over 20,000 descendants!

Male cats

There are sound reasons for having your male cat neutered. Apart from fathering unwanted kittens, entire males (toms) have the unpleasant habit of 'spraying' — marking their territory with pungent urine, the smell of which is very difficult to get rid of. They get involved in late-night fisticuffs with rival toms that wake up the entire neighbourhood. These cat-fights often result in wounds and abscesses, not to mention infection with deadly feline diseases. Amorous males roam far and wide in their quest for females in season and often get lost or killed on the road. Neutering will prevent all of these problems, with the bonus that your cat will be more affectionate and contented.

Female cats

There are equally sound reasons for having your female cat neutered. An entire female (queen) comes into season about once every three weeks for eight months of the year. She will cry incessantly and attract a host of noisy, smelly suitors to your door. Keeping her indoors to prevent her mating amounts to physical and mental cruelty as her strong biological urges are frustrated. If she escapes, she faces the same dangers as a tom when wandering in search of love, and if she mates with a tom that carries a serious feline disease she may be infected herself. And inevitably she will produce unplanned kittens for which you may have difficulty finding homes.

Above: *The ideal age for neutering a kitten is at five or six months old.*

It is a fallacy that it is kinder to allow female cats to have one litter of kittens before being spayed. A litter will not make them any more contented, nor will they live longer. In fact, mammary tumours and womb infections are far more common in cats who have had kittens, and some females that have a litter before being spayed remain broody for the rest of their lives.

So there you have it. Neutering makes life easier for you and your pet, and you can feel proud to have done your bit towards lessening the tragedy of unwanted animals.

Flea control

Even cats in the best circles may pick up fleas when outside the
house. Keeping one jump ahead of the flea problem requires a
two-pronged attack, regularly treating your home as well as your
cat. See page 111 for more information on flea prevention.

Worming

Regular worming will free your cat from potential intestinal
worms (see page 100). Wormers are available as tablets,
powders, liquids, granules and paste. They are sold in pet shops,
but the more effective products are available only from vets.
Frequency and dosage will depend on the type of product used.
As a guide, kittens from two to twelve weeks old should be
treated for roundworm every three weeks. Treat adult cats
for roundworm and tapeworm every three to six months.
Roundworm can be passed on from mother cat to kittens during
pregnancy and feeding. Ask your vet for advice on a safe wormer
for pregnant cats that won't damage the unborn kittens.

Cats often acquire tapeworm by swallowing fleas infected with
tapeworm larvae while grooming, so effective flea control is vital.

Dental hygiene

This area of preventative healthcare is easily overlooked by cat
owners, yet gum and tooth problems occur in eight out of every
ten cats over the age of three. Just like humans, cats tend to
accumulate plaque (a mixture of food debris and bacteria) on
their teeth. If left unchecked, plaque hardens to form calculus, or
tartar. This irritates the gums, causing gingivitis (see page 108),
and can even lead to tooth loss. The bacteria can also enter the
bloodstream and damage the kidneys and other organs.

Tooth brushing

Brushing your cat's teeth regularly from an early age can prevent dental problems from developing. Your vet can supply you with a soft brush or rubber fingertip applicator and special pet toothpaste (do not use toothpaste made for humans). You don't have to open the mouth to brush the teeth; simply pull back the gums. For those cats who hate anyone messing with their mouths, oral hygiene gels are available which can be given directly or mixed with the cat's food. They contain enzymes which inhibit the bacteria responsible for plaque formation. There are also dental chews and veterinary dried diets which contain fibrous matter that exerts a brushing action on the teeth as the cat chews. Giving your cat a chunk of tough meat to chew on once a week will also help to exercise his teeth and gums.

Dental inspection

Check your cat's teeth and gums regularly for signs of plaque (a yellowish or brownish coating on the teeth) and inflamed gums.

Take him to a vet, who will descale the teeth and, if necessary, remove any loose ones. Many cats appear amazingly rejuvenated after dental treatment, and cope well even after having a few teeth extracted.

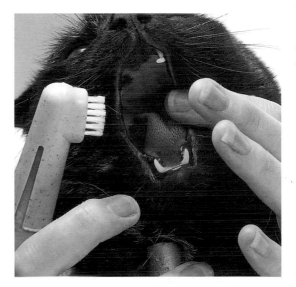

Right: *Open wide ... A soft-bristled rubber brush which fits on the end of your finger is the gentlest way to introduce your cat to the concept of toothbrushing.*

CHAPTER
FOUR

FEEDING YOUR CAT

The cat's natural diet — the mouse — provides all its nutritional needs in a neat, convenient package. It contains seventy per cent water, fourteen per cent protein, ten per cent fat and one per cent carbohydrate, plus vital minerals and trace elements. The liver is full of vitamins and the bones provide calcium and roughage.

Pet food manufacturers have re-invented the mouse, approximating the same formula and presenting it in an endless variety of forms and flavours. Kittens and seniors, fat cats and faddy cats, sick cats and healthy cats — all are catered for with diets specifically formulated for their individual needs.

Moist foods

Canned foods come in a wide variety of flavours and textures, but they vary in quality too. The cheaper brands are a false economy because they contain low-grade proteins and a high proportion of cereal. This means the cat needs to eat larger amounts to stay healthy. Always choose a good-quality brand with a protein level of about eight per cent. Canned foods contain 70–80 per cent moisture — about the same as in a cat's natural prey diet. Moist food is also available in foil pouches in convenient single-meal sizes. Keep opened cans covered and refrigerated, but bring them up to room temperature before serving. Most cats don't enjoy chilled food, probably because the aroma is 'locked in'.

Dog food should not be fed to cats as it is too low in protein and contains preservatives which may be harmful to them.

Did you know?

Experiments have shown that cats prefer their food at a temperature of 30°C (86°F), which happens to be the same temperature as freshly killed prey.

Dried foods

There are certain advantages to feeding complete dried foods.
They contain high-quality protein and the right balance of
nutrients and most cats find them very palatable. Their crunchy
texture also helps to keep cat's' teeth healthy. Dried foods are
more concentrated and thus higher in energy than canned
foods, so smaller servings are needed. This means that, weight
for weight, they are more economical than canned foods.
Another advantage is that they don't spoil, even in hot weather,
so there are no bad smells and food can be left available
throughout the day and your cat can choose his own meal times
(to avoid overfeeding, the daily amount recommended on the
packet should be weighed out accurately).

When buying dried foods, look for the word 'complete' on
the label. 'Complementary' foods are snack treats and should not

CHAPTER
FOUR

be served on a regular basis. The brands sold in supermarkets are perfectly adequate, but the premium-quality brands and special prescription diets are available only from vets and pet supply stores. As with canned foods, dried foods are available in different formulations suited to your cat's life stage, i.e. for kittens, adults and senior cats. If switching from a canned to a dried diet, gradually introduce the new food over a five to ten day period.

Did you know?

An adult cat requires forty different nutrients from its food. It also needs twice as much protein as a dog.

In the early days, dried diets contained high levels of magnesium, which produced a urine pH that was too alkaline, a cause of urinary tract disease in cats. This is no longer the case, and dry foods are perfectly safe in that respect. However, dried foods contain only about ten per cent moisture, so it is vital that plenty of fresh water is always available. If not, the cat's urine becomes reduced in volume and more concentrated, increasing the risk of urinary problems. If you are at all concerned, the solution may be to feed a mixed diet, perhaps giving canned food one day and dried the next.

Supplements and treats

Cats fed on a well-balanced diet do not need vitamin or mineral supplements; in fact, an excess can be harmful. Cat treats are not strictly necessary either. Some are of dubious nutritional value and feeding too many can lead to obesity.

Fresh foods

Your cat will enjoy the occasional treat of 'real' meat or fish for interest and variety. Try meals of raw, minced meat (pork must always be cooked) or lightly cooked fish, such as cod or coley.

Always remove the bones from poultry and fish as they splinter and sharp fragments could get stuck in your cat's throat. Some cats enjoy gnawing large cooked bones, such as lamb bones, and this provides exercise for the teeth and gums and allows the cat to indulge in natural 'hunting' behaviour.

Liver is a favourite with cats, but it should be restricted to a 50 g (2 oz) serving, no more than once a week. Liver is rich in vitamin A, which is essential to health, but an excess of this vitamin can cause serious bone disease. Liver is also high in magnesium, which can cause urinary tract problems.

Canned tuna, pilchards and sardines are quick and convenient meals, and highly nutritious. Some cats enjoy cheese, yogurt and scrambled eggs, and meals can be supplemented with a little cooked rice, pasta or potato, and cooked green vegetables.

No to vegetables

Please don't attempt to feed your cat a vegetarian diet. Cats are obligate carnivores, which means they must eat meat in order to survive. Unlike dogs, cats are unable to manufacture certain essential nutrients in their bodies, so it is vital that they are present in the cat's diet. The most important of these nutrients is an amino-acid called taurine, which is only found in animal tissue. Lack of taurine in the diet can lead to blindness, heart problems and eventual death. Vegetarianism is to be applauded, but inflicting your eating beliefs on your cat is cruel and irresponsible. Get a rabbit instead!

CHAPTER
FOUR

Milk

Contrary to popular belief, cats don't actually need milk once weaned. Some cats, notably Siamese and other Oriental breeds, cannot digest lactose (the sugar in cow's milk) and this causes diarrhoea. Special low-lactose feline milks are now available.

Water

Be sure your cat always has fresh water to drink. Frequent drinking will help keep his kidneys healthy and may help to reduce the risk of Feline urinary tract disease (FLUTD). Canned food contains up to eighty per cent moisture and will supply most of a cat's daily needs. However, a cat who is fed a dry diet, is elderly, has kidney disease, or is housebound will have a much greater need for water. Owners sometimes worry that their cat does not appear to drink much, but it is quite common for cats

Above: *The cat that got the cream! Cats are perverse creatures, and seem to enjoy a meal all the more if it has been begged, stolen or hunted.*

Grass

Cats occasionally nibble on grass, possibly as a way of obtaining moisture, roughage and valuable vitamins. Grass is also a natural emetic and helps to expel hairballs from the stomach. For cats which have no access to grass, pet shops sell trays of cocksfoot grass seed, which can be grown on a windowsill. This will discourage them from nibbling your houseplants, some of which are poisonous to cats.

to ignore their water bowl in favour of a puddle in the garden! Others seem to enjoy lapping from dripping taps and even the toilet bowl. To encourage your cat to drink water, serve it in a large bowl, preferably made of ceramic rather than plastic. Cats are sensitive to the chemicals in tap water, so leave it to stand for a while to allow the chemical smells to disperse.

How much, how often?

The dietary needs of your cat will vary depending on his age, health, temperament and activity levels. Follow the feeding guidelines given on the can or packet, but be flexible.

Pregnant and lactating cats

A pregnant cat needs extra food and nutrients to promote the healthy development of the kittens before birth and to help with milk production afterwards. During the last three weeks of pregnancy she will need up to twice her normal intake of food, and at least three times as much when she is feeding her young. She will also need extra fluids to replace those lost through producing milk. Continue the extra feeding until the kittens are weaned (at six to eight weeks). Then cut back gradually until she is eating her normal amount of food again.

Kittens

Starting at the age of three to four weeks, kittens can be gradually weaned on to solid food while still receiving milk from their mother. Try giving small helpings of boiled fish, finely minced chicken, scrambled egg and baby food. By the age of eight weeks, they should be fully weaned and eating solid food happily. Kittens grow rapidly and use up lots of energy in play. They need a high food intake, but their stomachs are tiny, so they require small, high-energy meals at frequent intervals. (No one would think of leaving a baby for eight hours without food, yet, surprisingly, some people do this to kittens!) At eight weeks old, a kitten will need a dessertspoonful of food five or six times a day. Gradually increase the size of the portions to two tablespoons per meal and reduce the number of feeds to four per day by six months old, when he can be fed adult-sized portions two or three times a day.

Food suitable for adult cats is too rich for kittens and can cause diarrhoea. Give a specially formulated kitten food. This is available in both canned and dried form and is high in protein, nutrients and energy, so it can be eaten in kitten-size portions and still provide all the nourishment needed during this important growth stage.

Adult cats

The average adult cat (from about nine months) will need half to two-thirds of a can of food per day. If you are giving him dried food, follow the guidance on the packet. In nature, cats prefer to eat little and often and if you are at home during the day there is good reason to indulge your pet in this way. Research shows that feeding several small meals, spaced throughout the day, helps to keep the cat's urine pH balance steady, reducing the risk of Feline lower urinary tract disease (FLUTD). Beware of overfeeding. Stick to the cat's daily ration and divide it into small portions. If you are away from home during the day, feed your cat in the morning and evening, or leave a bowl of dried food so he can eat at will.

Weight watching

Fat cats are on the increase — and we're not talking overpaid executives here! It is estimated that up to ten per cent of the UK's cats are overweight. While some well-fed cats are known to 'dine out' — pretending to be poor, hungry strays and cadging food from kindly neighbours — the majority do in fact eat sensibly. In most cases, it is we over-indulgent owners who are to blame for all those tubby tabbies. If we insist on offering irresistible titbits between meals, what self-respecting cat is going to refuse them? But we may be killing with kindness, because fat cats are more prone to develop diabetes, heart and respiratory problems, bladder stones and arthritis.

If you can't feel your cat's ribs for padding, or if there is a pouch of fat swinging between his back legs as he walks, get him checked by a vet to ensure there is no underlying health reason, such as an underactive thyroid. Otherwise, it's diet time. Your vet will prescribe a weight-reducing diet, which provides all the nutrients your cat needs to stay healthy while reducing the calorie content. Introduce the new food gradually, starting by mixing it in with the cat's normal food.

Be patient. A fat cat burns up less energy, so he needs less food to stay fat than a thin cat needs to stay thin. It can take a long time for the weight gain to reverse, and it is so tempting to give in when faced with a pair of big, imploring eyes! Of course, prevention is always easier than cure. If you start out with good eating habits from an early age and give your cat plenty of exercise, he will stay slim and trim.

KEEPING YOUR CAT SAFE

Our homes and gardens are full of potential dangers for a
playful, inquisitive kitten, and adult cats can get into scrapes,
too. Without being over-protective, you need to be aware of
potential dangers, just as you would with a child. A few
common-sense precautions can prevent serious accidents.

Indoor hazards

■ Check the washing machine and tumble drier before switching
them on. Cats are attracted to these warm, dark 'caves' and can
easily clamber in unnoticed.
■ Check cupboards, drawers, ovens, microwaves, fridges and
freezers before closing them.
■ Never give medicines intended for human use to your cat.
■ Avoid using disinfectants containing phenols or creosols
around the home as they are toxic to cats.
■ If you live in a flat, fit trellis or wire screens to balconies and
windows so your cat can enjoy fresh air in safety. Young cats in
particular are apt to fall when chasing an insect or bird. A DIY
enthusiast can easily make one from wood and chicken wire,
or you can buy window screen kits.
■ Don't leave needles and thread lying around. Cats seem to
be particularly fond of swallowing these, and the results can be
cat-astrophic if the thread gets wrapped around the intestines
or the needle punctures the stomach.
■ Keep electrical flexes out of harm's way as kittens are apt to
chew them. Unplug electrical appliances when not in use.
■ Remove any houseplants that are poisonous to cats, such as
poinsettia, ivy and azalea. Most adult cats will ignore them, but
kittens are susceptible as they chew anything and everything.

■ Keep cats out of the kitchen when you are cooking. Accidents often happen when a busy cook, carrying hot liquid, trips over a small animal moving around the kitchen. Ensure that the handles of saucepans do not project over the edge of the cooker.

■ Be attentive at bath time — a cat can fall into a bath of hot water or can be pushed in by a young child.

Above: *Some garden plants can present a hazard for inquisitive kittens.*

■ Cultivate the habit of looking before you step backwards, sit down or close a door. Because kittens are so quick and small they are apt to get underfoot and be trodden on accidentally.

Outdoor hazards

■ Never lock your cat out at night. Either keep him indoors or install a cat flap so he can come and go as he pleases.

■ Check garden sheds and garages before locking them in case your cat (or a neighbour's) has crept in unnoticed.

■ Antifreeze, oil and petrol are very toxic and cats can ingest them through licking their paws. Keep your garage clean!

■ Cover ponds, swimming pools and rain barrels with netting.

■ Keep your cat away from areas that have recently been sprayed with pesticides or weedkiller or painted with wood preservative. Even small quantities are harmful if swallowed when grooming or absorbed through the skin.

■ Make a habit of checking under your car, and under the bonnet, before starting up. Cats often use cars as shelter and can be accidentally run over or get trapped in the engine.

CHAPTER
FOUR

■ Repeated exposure to the sun can cause skin cancer of the nose or the ear tips, a particular problem with white cats. A dab of sunblock will protect on sunny days. (Cats sitting indoors on a sunny windowsill are safe from ultraviolet light.)

■ Keep your cat indoors on Bonfire Night. A cat terrified of exploding fireworks may run off and be lost or injured. He may also become the victim of an accident or a cruel prank.

▌Poisonous substances

In general, cats are careful about what they eat and unlikely to consume poisonous substances. Sadly, most cases of poisoning are caused unintentionally by owners who administer flea products wrongly or give their cat medicines intended for human use. Cats cannot metabolize certain compounds that are harmless to other animals; even an ordinary painkiller, such as aspirin, can cause severe vomiting, diarrhoea, convulsions and liver damage. A cat can also ingest poison if he licks his fur or his paws after contamination with household or garden chemicals, so always take great care when using these. Cats that hunt may unwittingly ingest dangerous amounts of rat poison by eating a rodent that has the bait in its stomach, and the results can be fatal.

The signs of poisoning depend on the substance ingested, but include

Left: *It is inadvisable to allow young cats to play in the kitchen, where many dangers lurk.*

severe vomiting and diarrhoea, loss of balance, muscle twitching, drooling, convulsions and collapse. Keep the cat in a quiet, darkened room and seek veterinary help urgently.

▌Indoors or out?

Cats have a wild streak and ideally they should be allowed to express their natural instincts to establish territory, climb trees, hunt for prey, socialize with other cats and snooze in the sun. However, we do not live in an ideal world and an outdoor cat is at risk of picking up diseases and parasites, getting lost or stolen, and injured or killed on the road. Whether to give a cat outdoor access or keep him permanently indoors is a dilemma

Above: *Cats are adept at climbing trees. However, they are not so good at getting down again!*

faced by all cat owners. In making your decision, you need to consider the environment you live in, your lifestyle and the character and age of your cat. Bear in mind also that once a cat has had some outdoor freedom he will resent being confined indoors thereafter and may develop behavioural problems, so make your decision early on and stick to it.

The outdoor cat

If you have a garden and live in a quiet area it is probably safe to install a cat flap and allow your cat to potter in and out during the day. Ideally the cat flap should be lockable so that you can keep your pet indoors at night, safe from the dangers of traffic and cat thieves. If you feel that free access is too risky, you could construct a large cat run in your garden, preferably linked to the house by a cat flap or a window. This will provide your cat with both safety and access to fresh air and sunshine. The run should have a warm, weatherproof section, and ideally be positioned in part sun and part shade. Equip it with a tree trunk or a climbing frame for the cat to scratch and climb on, some grass, perhaps a catnip plant, and of course a litter tray and water bowl, and your cat will be as happy as a sandboy. Climbing plants can be grown up the wire mesh to make the run more pleasing to the eye.

Alternatively you could 'cat-proof' your garden, in effect turning it into one large cat run, by enclosing it with a high fence curved inwards at the top using wire mesh attached to angled brackets so that the cat can't scale it. This has the added advantage of keeping unwanted feline intruders out.

The indoor cat

If you live in a flat or near a busy road it may be prudent to keep your cat indoors, especially if he is young (young cats are more likely to get lost or run into the road, while most adult cats develop a street-sense). Obviously it would be undesirable to keep a lively, energetic cat cooped up indoors if you are out at work all day. But if you choose the right cat (i.e., perhaps a kitten that has never experienced the outdoors, an elderly cat, or a placid, home-loving breed, such as a Persian) and if you can provide him with companionship, exercise and a stimulating environment, then there shouldn't be a problem.

You will need to provide your indoor cat with plenty of toys, a scratching post (if you value your furniture!) and ideally a climbing frame. Outdoor cats enjoy nibbling grass and drinking from ponds and puddles. Since your indoor cat will have access to neither of these, you should provide plenty of fresh drinking water and a tray of cocksfoot grass (available from pet shops) to aid digestion and help eliminate hairballs.

PLAY AND EXERCISE

Play is an important part of a cat's life, whether kitten or adult. Playing with your pet for just twenty minutes a day will give him physical and mental stimulation and strengthen the bond between you. Exercise is especially important for indoor cats so as to channel all the energy that they would normally use in patrolling territory and hunting prey. Indoor, inactive cats may become bored, lethargic and overweight and may express their frustration through behavioural problems.

Games

Anything that moves is appealing to a cat because it gives him a chance to hone his hunting skills. He likes nothing better than to chase a piece of string trailed across the floor or dangled enticingly in mid-air, and will even stalk a moving spot of light on a wall. Play 'cat-and-mouse' games with your cat, moving a toy in unpredictable ways and then stopping suddenly. Let him pounce, catch and 'kill' the toy before moving it again.

Left: *Play is a vital part of a cat's growing-up process. It tones the mind as well as the muscles, and helps alleviate boredom.*

CHAPTER
FOUR

Climbing frames

A multi-level climbing frame can be very therapeutic for indoor cats. These come in a range of sizes to suit your living space and incorporate sitting platforms, scratch-posts, tunnels and 'caves'. They offer cats the opportunity to stretch, climb, scratch and enjoy high vantage points from where they can safely observe their world, just as they would in nature.

Homespun fun

Pet shops offer all manner of sophisticated cat toys, but cats aren't fussy and will get just as much fun out of simple home-made toys. Variety is the key. Cats tend to get bored with a particular toy after a while, so it is a good idea to keep a selection in a box and bring out just one or two at a time.

■ Your cat will enjoy playing 'football' with a ping-pong ball or a crumpled ball of paper or aluminium foil.

■ Leave a large paper bag on the floor for him to dive into or rip to pieces (don't use plastic bags, and cut off any handles that could get caught around the cat's neck).

■ Seal up a large cardboard box and

cut holes in it big enough for your cat to jump through. Even better, glue several boxes together, linked by popholes, for kittens to play hide and-seek in.

■ Handy with a needle and thread? Make a pad or sack of fabric stuffed with some dried catmint, a herb which sends cats into transports of delight.

■ Make a 'fishing rod' toy out of a stick, a length of string, and a bunch of feathers or a wad of scrunched-up paper attached to the end of the string.

■ Make suppertime more fun by flicking nuggets of dried food across the kitchen floor for your cat to chase and eat.

The autumn years

Cats nowadays live longer, healthier lives than in the past. Thanks to advances in veterinary medicine, improved nutrition and effective vaccines, the average lifespan of a cat can extend well into his teens and even twenties. Cats age gracefully, and there is much you can do to ensure a happy and healthy 'retirement' for your loyal companion.

A twelve-year-old cat can be considered a pensioner as his age equates to a person of about seventy. As he ages, he will begin to slow down and spend more time snoozing in a warm spot. His hearing and eyesight gradually deteriorate and his joints become a little stiffer. His coat may lose some of its former glory and

Did you know?

A cat likes to feel secure when being picked up and should be held close to your body with one hand under the chest behind his front legs and the other under his bottom, supporting his weight. He should never be picked up by the scruff of the neck as this can cause him serious injury. Teach your children how to handle their pet, because if a cat is held incorrectly he will struggle to get free and may scratch and bite.

his eyes a little of their sparkle. You may notice him becoming thinner; he will also feel the cold more, so provide him with a cosy bed in a warm part of the house. If he is reluctant to go outside on cold days, put a litter tray indoors for him.

A very old cat may develop senility and will need to be kept safe and secure at all times. If he becomes confused he may wander off and get lost, or find a quiet place to die, and you will be left distraught at not knowing what has happened to him.

Feeding

As they age, cats are less able to digest the protein and fat in their diet, and need to eat more food to meet their daily energy requirements. Feeding small meals several times a day is better than two larger meals. You can buy 'senior' cat foods which contain high-quality protein and extra fat to compensate for reduced digestive function. Sardines in oil help prevent constipation, a condition to which elderly cats are prone. Fresh foods, such as rabbit, chicken and fish, are nourishing and easily digested.

Health care

Regular veterinary check-ups, every nine months or so depending on the cat's state of health, are advisable so that any health problems can be caught and treated early. Progressive kidney failure, for example, is common in older cats, and irreversible, but if it is diagnosed in the early stages it is possible to extend a cat's life with medication and a low-protein diet. The following are indications of serious health problems:

■ An increase in thirst and urination is a sure sign of liver or kidney problems, or diabetes.

How old is your cat?

Popular belief has it that one year of a cat's life is equivalent to seven human years. For a more accurate comparison, see the table below. Kittens mature at a faster rate than children, but they develop more slowly after two years.

Cat years	Human years
1	15
2	25
4	40
7	50
10	60
15	75
20	100

■ Bad breath and reluctance to eat can indicate gingivitis or kidney disease, or both. Check the teeth and gums, looking for yellow or brown scale, inflamed gums and mouth ulcers.

■ Difficulty in urinating indicates cystitis or Feline urinary tract disease (FLUTD).

Did you know?

Puss, a tabby cat from Devon, England, is reputed to be the world's oldest known cat. He died in 1939 the day after his thirty-sixth birthday.

The final curtain

When you love an animal very much it is natural to want to keep him alive at all costs. But if your cat has an untreatable condition and is suffering a great deal of pain or distress, you may have to consider having him put to sleep. It is not an easy thing to do, and grief is inevitably compounded by feelings of guilt. But remember that the final kindness you can offer your beloved companion is to allow him to pass away gently and with dignity.

The vet will administer a measured overdose of anaesthetic and your cat will quickly slip into a deep and permanent sleep with no pain or distress. Some owners elect to have their pet cremated and keep the ashes in a special container. Others choose to bury their pet in the garden.

It is natural to grieve over the death of a much-loved pet and you should not feel foolish or embarrassed about doing so. It may take months, even years, before you can think of your cat without that aching pang. You have been left with a cat-shaped gap in your life but lots of lovely memories to treasure.

CHAPTER FIVE

Cat health

*Ask any mother. A sick baby who can't tell you what's wrong
is a real worry – and the same applies to a sick pet. This
section looks at some of the most common cat ailments. It
tells you what signs to look out for, what action you need to
take, and how to help your cat back on the road to recovery.*

I f your cat displays any signs of illness, or any unusual
behaviour that causes you concern, you should take him
to the vet straight away. Don't delay. It is better to be safe
than sorry, and early diagnosis means less suffering for your
pet and a better chance of recovery if the illness or injury does
turn out to be serious.

A change in behaviour is often
the first sign of a health problem.
A normally active cat with a
good appetite will appear
depressed and lethargic and
refuse to eat. The problem could
be as simple as worms, a hairball
or constipation, but it
may be a warning
sign of something
more serious so get it
checked out and don't be
afraid to ask your vet for advice.

THE SIGNS OF ILLNESS

It is important to recognise when your cat is unwell, and to know when a problem is potentially serious so you can get veterinary help quickly. This chart will help you identify the possible cause of a cat's illness, but it is intended only as a guide. Often a symptom may have more than one cause and proper diagnosis can only be made by a qualified vet.

Symptoms	Possible cause
■ Vomiting	
Cat vomits up a sausage-shaped ball of hair	Hairball (p.99)
Mild vomiting, no other symptoms	Minor stomach upset; worms (p.100); milk intolerance
Yellow or brown liquid accompanied by diarrhoea, lethargy	Feline enteritis (p.103); poisoning (p.125)
■ Eating and drinking	
Cat appears thirsty but refuses to drink	Feline infectious enteritis (p.103)
Excessive thirst	Kidney disease (p.118); feline leukaemia (p.94); diabetes (p.104)
Cat appears hungry but eats only small amounts	Hairball (p.99)
■ Weight	
Sudden weight loss, accompanied by increased thirst and urination	Kidney disease (p.118)
Gradual weight loss plus increased appetite and thirst, hyperactivity	Hyperthyroidism (p.96)
Abdomen appears distended but back is thin	Feline infectious peritonitis (p.102); tumour
■ Eyes	
Third eyelid visible	General sign of ill-health; worms (p.100)
Clear or thick discharge plus sneezing, lethargy, loss of appetite	Cat flu (p.109); sinusitis
Eyelids red and sore plus discharge	Conjunctivitis (p.105); chlamidiosis (p.105); entropion (p.105)

Symptoms	Possible cause
■ Ears	
Persistent scratching and head-shaking plus dark brown wax in ear canal	Ear mites (p.107); canker of ear
Large blood-blister on ear flap	Haematoma (p.107)
■ Mouth	
Drooling; bad breath; red and inflamed gums; brown tartar on teeth; difficulty in eating	Gingivitis (p.108)
Drooling; reluctance to eat; pawing at mouth; breathing difficulties	Foreign body stuck in mouth or throat (p.126); poisoning (p.125); cat flu (p.109)
Abnormally pale gums	Anaemia (p.94); if cat is injured, may be shock (p.125)
Chronic gingivitis plus weight loss and recurring infections	Feline immunodeficiency virus (FIV) (p.95)
■ Nose	
Sneezing	Cat flu (p.109); allergy; grass seed lodged in nose; sinusitis
Nose feels wet; discharge; sneezing; lethargy, lack of appetite	Cat flu (p.109)
■ Skin and coat	
Balding patches and broken hairs	Ringworm (p.116); hormonal disease
Large, raised swelling, possibly exuding pus; cat depressed, refuses to eat	Abscess (p.116)
Small whitish or greyish bean-shaped swelling; cat appears normal	Ticks (p.114)
Persistent scratching; presence of tiny black specks in coat	Fleas (p.111)
Pinkish lesions on skin	Flea allergy (p.115)
■ Anal area	
Persistent licking of anal area	FLUTD (p.118)
Smeared with faeces	Diarrhoea (p.98)
White 'grains of rice' visible in fur around anus or in stools	Tapeworm (p.100)

BLOOD AND GLANDULAR DISORDERS

Anaemia

This is not a disease itself but a sign of an underlying problem in which the number of circulating red blood cells, and/or the amount of haemoglobin, and the amount of oxygen carried in the blood, are reduced. There are three main reasons why this arises. They are as follows:

■ Reduced production of red blood cells due to poisoning, chronic kidney disease or Feline leukaemia.

■ Destruction of red blood cells due to Feline infectious anaemia.

■ Loss of blood due to either an external or internal injury, a bleeding ulcer or tumour, a chronic infestation of blood-sucking parasites, or ingestion of warfarin, a rodenticide which prevents blood clotting.

■ **Symptoms:** These include breathlessness, lethargy, pale eye and mouth membranes and loss of appetite. Anaemic cats often eat earth or other unnatural materials.

Treatment: Consult a vet immediately if you notice any signs of anaemia. A blood test will confirm diagnosis. Treatment will depend on the cause.

Feline leukaemia virus (FeLV)

This is an often fatal virus that breaks down the cat's immune system, lowering its resistance to other infections. It is contagious and is spread by exposure to an infected cat's saliva or blood, usually by fighting, mating and mutual grooming. It can also be passed on to kittens in the womb or via the mother's milk. Young cats are most susceptible to infection, although the incubation period for the disease can be up to three years. Some cats shrug off the virus and develop an immunity. A small number become symptomless carriers. The less lucky ones develop FeLV-related symptoms.

■ **Symptoms:** These include poor appetite, weight loss, anaemia, intermittent fever, breathing difficulties and enlarged lymph nodes. Some cats develop malignant tumours.

Treatment: There is no cure for FeLV. If your cat has anaemia or suffers from recurrent infections, he should be blood-tested for FeLV. If he tests positive, he should be isolated from other cats until he has been re-tested. If he then tests negative, he has developed immunity. If he remains positive but does not show any symptoms, there is no reason why he cannot live on to advanced years, but he can still shed the virus and infect other cats, so he must be isolated. The virus dies rapidly outside the body and is easily killed by disinfectants. An effective vaccine is now available for FeLV, but it is advisable to do a blood test first to determine whether the cat is already infected. Any new cat that is introduced to the household should also be blood-tested to ensure that it is not a carrier.

Feline immunodeficiency virus (FIV)

FIV is similar to HIV, the cause of AIDS in people, but it only affects cats and cannot be transmitted to humans. The virus is fragile and dies very quickly outside the body, so it cannot be transmitted indirectly. It is mainly transmitted by bite wounds, so is more common in male cats than females, and especially in entire tom cats who regularly get into fights. Like FeLV, the virus attacks the immune system.

■ **Symptoms:** These are similar to those of FeLV (see page 94). FIV is particularly associated with chronic gingivitis (see page 108). Many FIV-positive cats can remain healthy for years before secondary infections become apparent.

Treatment: Any cat suffering from recurring infections should be blood-tested for FIV. No vaccine exists, nor is there a cure; treatment is merely supportive. Oil of evening primrose has been shown to have a beneficial effect on FIV-positive cats. An infected cat which is aggressive is a serious threat to healthy cats and must be isolated. All new cats that are introduced into a household should first be tested for FIV.

Feline infectious anaemia (FIA)

This disease is caused by an infectious blood parasite that damages the cat's red blood cells, causing severe anaemia. It is thought to be transmitted by blood-sucking insects, such as fleas, ticks and mosquitos.

■ **Symptoms:** These include lethargy, weight loss and pale gums.

Treatment: A blood test will confirm FIA. Treatment involves antibiotics, iron supplements and, in severe cases, blood transfusions.

Hyperthyroidism

This is a common condition in older cats, due to an over-active thyroid gland. Hyperthyroidism puts a strain on the heart and kidneys which can eventually prove fatal.

■ **Symptoms:** These are very subtle at first, but in time you will notice a marked increase in appetite and thirst, hyperactivity, weight loss, rapid heart rate and a dull coat.

Treatment: Diagnosis is through a blood test, or by feeling the enlarged thyroid gland in the throat. The gland can be surgically reduced in size, but the condition may recur within a few years. If the cat is too old or weak to risk an operation he can be given drugs to reduce the output of thyroid hormone. Some specialist veterinary centres can combat the condition using injections of radioactive iodine to destroy the abnormal thyroid tissue. Some cats respond well to homoeopathic treatment of this condition.

DIGESTIVE AND ABDOMINAL PROBLEMS

Vomiting

Cats often vomit, usually to rid themselves of hairballs. If the vomiting is frequent and accompanied by other signs, such as diarrhoea, loss of appetite and lethargy, this can be a symptom of a more serious problem. Consult a vet immediately. Cats that eat too quickly often

Right: *To combat dehydration, provide plenty of water, but no milk.*

regurgitate their food soon after eating. Persistent regurgitation may indicate a disease or blockage of the oesophagus and warrants veterinary advice.

Treatment: Withhold food and encourage the cat to drink water to avoid dehydration. Do not give milk. Once the vomiting has subsided, feed a bland diet of white meat or fish, mixed with a little rice, for the next twenty-four hours.

Diarrhoea

Mild diarrhoea may be due to unsuitable foods, an abrupt change of diet, bacterial infection, worms or allergy to cow's milk. Severe cases may be due to food-poisoning, feline enteritis or liver disease and can lead to dehydration. If the diarrhoea is persistent, contains blood, or is accompanied by vomiting, consult your vet. Diarrhoea in kittens is usually due to worms, incorrect feeding, or a microscopic parasite called Giardia.

Treatment: Starve the cat for a few hours to allow the stomach to rest, then introduce small amounts of cooked chicken or fish. Provide plenty of fresh water but withhold milk. Worms can be treated with a veterinary worming preparation, and Giardia with special anti-protozoal drugs.

Constipation

This condition may be due to a hairball blocking the cat's bowel. Elderly cats that are inactive can sometimes suffer from constipation due to loss of muscle tone in the bowel.

■ **Symptoms:** The cat appears lethargic and will strain to pass a motion. It is important to differentiate between straining caused by constipation and straining due to urinary obstruction, which is a very serious condition.

Treatment: Dose the cat with liquid paraffin. If the symptoms persist, seek veterinary advice.

Hairball

This is an accumulation of hair in the stomach as a result of constantly licking the coat while grooming. Normally the cat will eat grass and vomit up the hairball (as a matted ball of hair) but if it becomes too large it can form a blockage in the bowel, causing recurrent vomiting and digestive problems. A cat with hairballs will make frequent trips to his food bowl but consume only a small amount at a time.

Above: *When a cat is seen eating grass, he is probably attempting to remove a hairball from his stomach.*

Treatment: Feed an oily fish, such as sardines or mackerel, once a week to ease the passage of hairballs. There are malt-flavoured hairball remedies which taste attractive to cats. Another remedy is olive oil or liquid paraffin: give one teaspoon per day for three days. Regular grooming helps to prevent hairballs.

Worms

The most common intestinal parasites in cats are roundworms and tapeworms. They are not blood-suckers but feed on semi-digested food within the stomach and intestines. Cats that hunt, and those with fleas, are more likely to catch worms.

Roundworms

Mature roundworms look like thin, white garden worms. Their eggs pass out in the cat's faeces and are then eaten by a rodent, bird or insect. If a cat eats this intermediate host, the eggs develop into adult worms in the cat's intestine and the cycle is completed. Kittens can also be infected in their mother's womb or via her milk. Adult cats seldom show any signs of roundworm infection, but there are clear signs in kittens.

■ **Symptoms:** These include a dull coat, coughing, vomiting, diarrhoea and a characteristic pot-bellied appearance caused by accumulation of worms and gas in the intestines.

Treatment: Kittens from six weeks upwards should be dosed regularly against roundworms; ask your vet for a suitable preparation.

Tapeworms

Tapeworms are most often found in adult cats. The worm's head fastens on to the gut wall. The long, flat body consists of egg-filled segments that break off and pass out in the faeces. The segments then release their eggs into the environment. Tapeworms are not spread directly from cat to cat but via an intermediate host.

The host for one species of tapeworm is the cat flea, and for another it is small rodents or birds. If a cat eats infected prey, or swallows an infected flea during grooming, the worm larvae hatch out in the gut, where they mature into adult tapeworms

Right: *Free-roaming cats, especially those that hunt,* are more likely to become infected with worms. Regular worming is advisable.

and the cycle begins again.

■ **Symptoms:** Cats can have tapeworms without showing any symptoms, but a heavy infestation can cause weight loss and poor condition, digestive upsets and anal irritation. Segments, which look like small grains of rice, may be seen sticking to the fur around the anus or in the stools.

Treatment: Infestation can be avoided by worming your cat regularly and keeping him free of fleas (see page 111).

Other types of worm

The following internal parasites are less common.

■ **Lungworms:** These are not common and the cat may show no symptoms apart from coughing in order to expel the worms.

■ **Whipworms:** These tiny, thin, blood-sucking worms live in the cat's large intestine.

■ **Threadworms:** These live in the small intestine, where they burrow into the gut wall and may cause haemorrhages.

■ **Hookworms:** These blood-sucking worms are more common in Australia and the United States. They live in the small intestine.

■ **Heartworms:** These occur only in hot, humid countries and are spread by mosquitoes. They may block off the circulation, causing sudden death, or cause circulatory disorders.

Toxoplasmosis

This is an illness that causes much concern, thanks to alarmist talk in the press about its connection with cats and its effects on pregnant women. Cats pick up the intestinal parasite, *Toxoplasma gondii*, by eating infected prey or raw meat, but rarely show signs of illness. Similarly, most humans have contracted toxoplasmosis at some time – by handling raw meat or eating undercooked meat – the only symptoms being, at worst, a mild form of flu.

The problem arises if a pregnant woman contracts the disease, as there is a slight risk of birth defect in her unborn child. The reason cats get a bad press is because the parasite eggs are shed in their faeces and so, in theory, humans can become infected by handling contaminated cat faeces.

However, the risk is extremely small because, frankly, who in their right mind is going to handle cat faeces and then put their hand in their mouth? Infection is far more likely if you handle or eat infected meat or soil-covered vegetables. Nevertheless, to be on the safe side, pregnant women should wear gloves when gardening and cleaning the litter tray, avoid eating rare meat, and always wash their hands after handling raw meat.

Feline infectious peritonitis (FIP)

This insidious disease, which is thankfully rare, is caused by a feline coronavirus. It mainly attacks cats under three years of age; older cats generally have a natural immunity. FIP is transmitted via infective faeces and saliva and the risk is greater in large groups of cats sharing the same feeding bowls and litter tray. A cat may be infected by another cat who is a healthy carrier of the virus. A blood test cannot detect the virus itself, but it does detect the blood titre level (the level of antibodies to coronavirus in the blood). Whereas in most diseases a high antibody level is beneficial, with coronavirus the opposite is true and a high antibody level is cause for concern. The good news is that ninety per cent of cats with coronavirus antibodies do not go on to develop FIP. The bad news is that most cats who do develop FIP will die within weeks.

■ **Symptoms:** FIP is difficult to diagnose because the early symptoms — fever, lethargy, weight loss and poor appetite — are typical of many other feline diseases. Within days, weeks or months, the cat will go on to develop one of two variants of FIP: in the 'wet' form, fluid accumulates in the abdomen, which appears grossly distended. Fluid may also form in the cat's chest, causing laboured breathing. The 'dry' form of FIP can affect the nervous system, causing fits, loss of balance, paralysis or urinary incontinence. Bleeding into the front of the eye is another sign of dry FIP.

Treatment: No vaccine is currently available in the UK, nor is there any effective treatment (although homoeopathy is said to be effective in relieving the symptoms). An infected cat must be isolated from other cats. The virus dies outside the feline body within 48 hours, and is destroyed by disinfectants.

▌Feline infectious enteritis (FIE)

Also known as Feline panleucopaenia, FIE is a serious viral infection of the intestines, mainly affecting kittens and young cats. The virus is highly contagious and is spread by direct or indirect contact with an infected cat. The illness is sudden in onset and young kittens may die before a diagnosis can be made.

■ **Symptoms:** These are varied, but include fever, loss of appetite, vomiting (usually a bright yellow liquid) and profuse diarrhoea. The cat sits hunched over his water bowl but doesn't drink. He may cry out due to abdominal pain. Kittens infected in the womb suffer brain damage and develop a staggering gait.

Treatment: See your vet immediately; the cat may recover if treated promptly. Keep him isolated from other pets. This virus is very tough and can remain in the environment for up to a year, so ask your vet for advice on disinfecting your home. Discourage visits to and from other cat-owners' homes, as the virus can be carried on clothing and footwear. Fortunately there is an effective vaccine against this disease.

Diabetes

This is a condition caused by inadequate production of insulin by the pancreas. There are two types of diabetes that affect cats.
■ **Diabetes mellitus:** Mostly affects older cats, and obese cats run double the normal risk. The symptoms are excessive drinking and urinating, lethargy and increased appetite. Another tell-tale sign is a 'pear-drop' odour on the breath. Cataracts may develop.
■ **Non-insulin dependent diabetes:** Cats that are very overweight can develop a type of diabetes called non-insulin dependent diabetes. In this case, the body cannot respond to its own insulin due to the stress of carrying so much excess weight.

Treatment: A blood or urine test will confirm diagnosis. Diabetic cats require lifelong treatment with insulin injections to control their blood glucose levels. If the underlying weight problem is treated with dietary therapy, the amount of insulin required is less. In the case of non-insulin dependent diabetes, if the cat's weight drops to normal he may no longer need injections at all.

EYE AND EAR PROBLEMS

Conjunctivitis

This is an inflammation of the membranes of the eyes, causing them to appear red and swollen with a watery or mucoid discharge. If both eyes are affected it may be a symptom of cat flu, a bacterial infection such as chlamidya, or an allergy. If only one eye is affected it may be due to a fight wound or an object such as a grass seed in the eye. Watering or discharge of the eyes can also be caused by a condition called entropion (see below).

Treatment: Gently bathe the eyes with warm boiled water. Consult your vet, who will treat the cause and prescribe eye drops.

Entropion

A rare condition in which the eyelid is 'rolled in', and the cornea is constantly irritated by the lashes.
■ **Symptoms:** Excessive tear production and discharge.

Treatment: Surgical correction of the eyelid is required.

Right: *An overproduction of tears is often caused by blocked tear ducts, and is fairly common in Persians due to narrow tear ducts and the short nose produced by breeding. Gently bathe the eyes with warm water.*

The third eyelid

The cat is unusual in that it has a third eyelid — the haw, or nictitating membrane — at the inner corner of each eye. The third eyelids are not visible in a healthy cat, but when they protrude, looking like white curtains partly drawn across the eyes, it can indicate a health problem such as cat flu or worm infestation.

Often, it is due to infection with a harmless retrovirus which affects the nerves that control the nictitating membrane. The cat may develop diarrhoea, but otherwise remains healthy. The eyes return to normal eventually, although this can take several weeks.

Cataracts

An uncommon condition, sometimes seen in elderly or diabetic cats.
■ **Symptoms:** The lens of the eye becomes cloudy and opaque, resulting in partial or complete loss of vision.

Treatment: Surgery may be necessary if both eyes are affected.

Glaucoma

Most common in elderly cats, glaucoma occurs when there is increased pressure within the eyeball, caused by inflammation, internal bleeding or a tumour.
■ **Symptoms:** The eye appears enlarged and cloudy.

Treatment: This is a painful and serious condition requiring prompt veterinary attention.

Ear mites

Tiny mange mites are present in most cats' ears, particularly in those of kittens.
■ **Symptoms:** Severe infestation causes intense irritation and excessive production of dark brown wax. This makes the cat scratch or shake his ears persistenly, causing inflammation and possibly a haematoma (see below).

Treatment: Your vet will clean the ears and prescribe ear drops. These kill the adult mites but not their eggs, so the drops must be used for twenty-one days in order to eradicate the problem. Ear mites are very contagious, so treat all cats and dogs in the household.

Haematoma

Fighting or persistent scratching due to ear mites can rupture blood vessels in the ear flap.
■ **Symptoms:** A large blood blister or haematoma. If left untreated, the fluid becomes absorbed into the ear flap and causes permanent crinkling of the ear.

Treatment: Consult your vet, who will drain off the fluid. Check for ear mites and treat these as well.

Warning

On no account should you poke a cat's ears with tweezers or cotton wool buds as serious and painful damage can occur.

MOUExT PROBLEMS

(MOUTH PROBLEMS)

Gingivitis

This condition is usually caused by a build-up of tartar on the teeth which pushes back on the gums, causing them to become inflamed and sore.

■ **Symptoms:** The first sign of gingivitis is often a dark red line along the gum margin. Then the gums become spongy, red and sore. Other signs are dribbling, bad breath and difficulty in eating. In association with other symptoms, chronic gingivitis can signify kidney failure or diseases such as diabetes mellitus, Feline leukaemia virus and Feline immunodeficiency virus.

Treatment: Consult a vet, who will determine the underlying cause and remove the tartar under anaesthetic. See page 70 for information on routine dental care for your cat.

Right: *Gingivitis can be a painful and debilitating condition in cats. There are several causes of the condition, including viral infection and an allergy to plaque on the teeth.*

Ulcers

Red, ulcerated areas on a cat's tongue are a symptom of cat flu. Ulcers on the gums can indicate kidney disease. An open sore on the cat's upper lip is a 'rodent ulcer', the cause of which is not known. The ulcer will both enlarge and deepen if left untreated, although the condition is not malignant.

Treatment: If caught early, your vet should be able to stop the ulcer spreading across the face by using drugs and perhaps cryosurgery (deep cold treatment).

RESPIRATORY PROBLEMS

Feline respiratory disease ('cat flu')

Most cases of cat flu are caused by one of two viruses:
■ Feline viral rhinotracheitis (FVR)
■ Feline calcivirus (FCV).
Both are highly contagious and can be spread either directly, by breathing in infective droplets, or indirectly through shared food bowls or litter trays. FVR is the more serious disease, with symptoms including apathy, fever, loss of appetite, sneezing, breathing difficulties and a heavy discharge from the eyes and nose. There may be painful mouth ulcers which cause excessive salivation and difficulty in eating. Even after recovery, cats can, when under stress, continue to shed the virus and infect others for up to eleven months. Others may be left with recurrent rhinitis (runny nose). The symptoms of FCV are similar but usually milder.
■ Another cause of respiratory disease is chlamydia, an infection

caused by an organism which is a hybrid of a virus and a bacterium. It produces mild symptoms, such as conjunctivitis and nasal discharge.

Treatment: Cat flu can be fatal, especially in kittens, so take your cat to a vet as soon as symptoms appear. He may prescribe antibiotics and a nasal decongestant. Isolate the cat from other pets, and warn other cat owners to stay away until the infection is completely cleared. Good home nursing is essential. Keep the eyes and nose clean by bathing them with warm water, which has been lightly salted. Keep a close watch on the cat's breathing; if he is having difficulties, seek veterinary help. Vaccines are available to protect against cat flu and chlamydia.

Asthma

As in humans, asthma in the cat is commonly caused by an allergic reaction to inhaled substances: pollen and house dust mite faeces.
■ **Symptoms:** These are wheezing and coughing.

Treatment: Your vet may prescribe steroidal anti-inflammatory drugs for your cat.

Lungworm

This tiny parasite may be found in the lungs of cats in rural areas. It is uncommon and infection usually goes unnoticed.

Treatment: The cat may cough up parasites and get rid of them, otherwise a vet can prescribe a specific remedy.

SKIN AND COAT PROBLEMS

Fleas

It is not just cats who enjoy the benefits of modern living — their fleas also thrive in our close-carpeted, centrally-heated homes. Most cats are troubled with fleas at some time or another; they pick them up from other cats, from dogs, and even from the garden.

■ **Symptoms:** Persistent scratching is often the most obvious sign of flea infestation. Fleas are dark brown in colour and 1–2 mm long; you may find them in the cat's coat during combing, as well as tiny black specks of flea dirt. The peak season for fleas is late summer, when high humidity and high temperatures enable them to breed rapidly.

Fleas spread disease

Fleas are not just an itchy nuisance; they can also cause health problems. In young kittens, a heavy infestation can cause anaemia which is potentially life-threatening. Fleas act as intermediate hosts for certain tapeworms and are believed to be carriers of feline infectious anaemia. Some cats become sensitive to flea saliva in bites and develop allergic dermatitis, an itchy, scabby reaction which can cause great discomfort. Fleas sometimes bite people, too!

CHAPTER
FIVE

Treatment of flea infestation

In order to control fleas it helps to understand their life cycle. Adult fleas can live for seven to fourteen days and remain permanently on your pet, feeding and reproducing. The females lay many eggs a day which fall to the ground. The eggs hatch into tiny larvae that burrow into carpets and upholstery. There they develop into pupae, which can remain dormant for many months awaiting the arrival of a suitable host. When they sense warmth and vibration, the adult fleas emerge and leap onto a passing cat (or dog) to start the whole life cycle again.

For every flea living on your cat there could be ninety-nine developing fleas lurking in your home, so it is important to treat the environment as well as the cat (and any dogs in the household). In the past, flea control products were messy, smelly, difficult to use and often toxic, but modern products are safer, and more effective because they not only kill adult fleas but also prevent the development of eggs and larvae, thus preventing re-infestation.

Treating the cat: Various types of anti-flea preparations are now available. However, the most effective ones are available only from vets.

■ **Oral suspensions** are very effective and safe enough to be given to weaned kittens and pregnant cats. A liquid dose containing an insect growth inhibitor is given by mouth once a month (now also available as a six-monthly injection by your vet). When a flea bites the cat it ingests the compound and is effectively sterilized, stopping the flea life cycle in its tracks. This method will not kill existing fleas, so you may need to use a topical insecticide before starting the treatment.

Left: *Oral preparations can be given with your cat's food.*

■ **Drop-ons** are very easy to use. A small pipette of liquid is applied to the skin at the back of the cat's neck once a month. It spreads over the body surface, killing fleas before they can lay new eggs. The non-organophosphate compound is safe for you and your cat.

■ **Aerosols:** Most cats dislike the noise these make, although pump-action sprays are quieter. Some sprays are alcohol-based, so keep the cat away from heat sources such as fires and hot ovens until the coat is dry.

■ **Flea collars** dispense insecticide over a period of several months. However, these are now less popular as the cat is constantly in contact with the insecticide. Make sure the collar is elasticated and check underneath for any signs of skin inflammation.

■ **Powders** are also losing popularity as they are messy, cats hate them and they are less effective than the more modern treatments now available.

Treating the home: Regular
vacuum-cleaning will remove most of the eggs and immature fleas from carpets and upholstery. For total protection there are environment sprays that kill the emerging fleas, and some also contain an insect growth regulator which prevents the eggs from hatching.

Use pesticides safely

Cats are susceptible to the toxic effects of insecticides because of their grooming habits.

■ Always follow the manufacturer's instructions carefully when using any anti-flea treatment.

■ Check that the product is safe for use on kittens.

■ Only one type of insecticide should be used on a cat at any one time. For example, do not use both a flea collar and a flea spray.

■ Never use an environment spray, or a spray for use on dogs, on your cat as poisoning will occur.

■ Avoid spraying your cat within several days of worming as the two treatments together can prove toxic.

■ Avoid spraying your cat for a few days after he has received a general anaesthetic.

■ Cover fish tanks and remove caged birds, food and water bowls when spraying the room against fleas.

■ Keep children away from treated animals until the fur is dry.

■ Consult your vet immediately if your cat shows a bad reaction to a flea product, such as convulsions or excess salivation.

Ticks

In rural areas in particular, cats may pick up ticks when walking in long grass. The tick buries its head deep into the cat's skin, where it feeds off blood.

■ **Symptoms:** An engorged tick looks like a small, blue-grey bean and because it doesn't move is often mistaken for a tumour or cyst. A heavy infestation may cause anaemia. In Australia, certain ticks secrete a toxin that causes paralysis.

Treatment: Do not attempt to pull a tick out as the head may be left behind, causing an abscess. A simple remedy is to cover it with petroleum jelly and just leave it alone. The tick will die of suffocation and fall off, with mouth parts intact, within twenty-four hours. Alternatively, squirt it with flea spray.

Mites

These minute skin parasites can cause itching and hair loss.

■ **Fur mites** (also known as 'walking dandruff') are highly contagious and look like dandruff along the cat's back.

■ **Harvest mites,** or 'chiggers', are visible in autumn as tiny orange-red spots between the cat's toes or in the folds of the ears.

Treatment: Spray the cat with an ordinary flea preparation.

Lice

Lice are far less common than fleas, and affect rural cats more than urban ones. Cats with lice infection are very itchy.

■ **Symptoms:** The louse is a pinhead-sized, light grey, slowly

Right: *When using flea sprays, hold the can at a safe distance and spray against the lie of the fur and away from the face. Pump-action sprays are less frightening for your cat than aerosol sprays.*

moving insect. You will also see the translucent eggs, which look like dandruff but are firmly glued to the cat's hairs.

Treatment: Flea sprays kill adult lice but not the eggs. Spray the cat once a week for at least three weeks in order to kill the young lice as they hatch. As the eggs remain on the cat it is not necessary to spray the whole house, as with flea infestation.

Allergic dermatitis

This is an inflammation of the skin, most often triggered by sensitivity to flea saliva (see page 111). Some cats develop allergic reactions to even a single bite.

■ **Symptoms:** Excessive grooming is a common sign, and small scabs may appear, especially on the back.

Treatment: Evening primrose oil can help reduce the skin's sensitivity, but corticosteroids may be prescribed in severe cases. A food supplement called spirulina, available from health food shops, has been shown to be successful in treating some skin problems.

Abscesses

Cats have a lot of bacteria on their teeth, which is why a bite from another cat often results in an abscess. The puncture wound made by the sharp canine teeth is deep, but the opening on the surface is very small and soon closes, leaving infection trapped deep down. A hot, painful swelling results, and the cat becomes listless and off his food and may also have a high temperature. The areas around the neck and the base of the tail are common sites for abscesses. If the side of the face is swollen it may indicate a tooth abscess.

Treatment: Do not attempt to lance the abscess but bathe it frequently with hand-hot water, lightly salted. This will bring the abscess to a head and after twenty-four hours it should burst, emitting green, blood-stained pus. Once this happens, your cat will feel more comfortable. Continue bathing and gently squeezing to drain all the pus and to prevent the abscess re-forming. If it does not burst within twenty-four hours, contact your vet, who will open and drain the abscess and prescribe a course of antibiotics to clear the infection. An untreated abscess can lead to blood poisoning.

Ringworm

This is a highly contagious fungal infection which can be caught from an infected cat, rat or mouse, or via an object harbouring the spores. The fungus invades the surface of the skin and weakens the hair shaft, causing it to break off.
■ **Symptoms:** The signs of ringworm vary, but classically they are small, round, scaly bald patches, usually on the head,

Ringworm and humans

Ringworm is transmissible to humans. Though healthy adults are normally unaffected, children, the elderly and adults with a low immune system are vulnerable. See your doctor if any circular red patches appear on the skin, particularly on the hands or arms.

ears, forelegs or paws. In some cases the only sign is a few broken hairs, and some cats carry ringworm without showing any symptoms at all.

Treatment: Diagnosis can be confirmed using an ultra-violet Woods Light and possibly microscopic and culture tests. A long course of Griseofulvin, an anti-fungal drug, will be required. An infected cat must be isolated from other cats, as well as dogs and children, until treatment is completed. Always wash your hands thoroughly after handling the cat. The fungal spores remain infectious in the household for a long time. Ask your vet for advice on clearing the infection.

Fly-strike

Old, injured and sick cats are vulnerable to fly-strike in summer. Blowflies lay their eggs on an infected wound or on soiled hair. When the maggots hatch they feed on the cat's flesh and release a toxin into the bloodstream which can rapidly prove fatal.

Treatment: Fly-strike is a serious condition. Rush the cat to a vet, who will remove the maggots (not a job for the squeamish!), clean the wound and prescribe antibiotics.

CHAPTER
FIVE

URINARY TRACT DISORDERS

Kidney disease

Many older cats suffer from kidney problems. As normal kidney tissue is replaced with scar tissue, the kidneys become less efficient at filtering waste products out of the blood. The disease progresses very slowly over weeks to months.

■ **Symptoms:** The first warning signs are a dull coat, increased thirst, gradual weight loss and more frequent urination. In advanced cases there is lethargy, lack of appetite, vomiting, ulcers in the mouth and a smell of ammonia on the breath.

Treatment: Diagnosis is made by blood tests. Your vet will suggest a special diet with moderately restricted levels of high-quality, easily digested protein and low levels of phosphorous and sodium, designed to reduce the strain on the kidneys. Steroids may be given to boost the appetite. Water must be freely available at all times to satisfy increased thirst and stimulate the kidneys to function. With early detection and careful management, the progress of the disease can be slowed down and your cat can live quite happily for several more years.

Feline lower urinary tract disease (FLUTD)

FLUTD is triggered by the formation of crystals (mineral deposits) within the cat's urinary system. It is a potentially serious condition as the accumulation of crystals can completely block the urethra (the tube that carries urine from the bladder to the outside) so that the cat is unable to urinate. It is more common in male cats as they have a narrower urethra than females.

■ **Symptoms:** The cat strains frequently to pass small drops of urine, which may contain blood. He may cry out in pain and persistently lick his rear end. It is important not to confuse these symptoms with constipation as urethral obstruction is a life-threatening condition that needs urgent treatment. When urine cannot be passed, the bladder soon fills up to capacity and may rupture, releasing the contents into the abdominal cavity, and the cat could die from shock and peritonitis.

Treatment: There are two forms of urinary crystals: struvite, which tend to form when the cat's urine is too alkaline, and calcium oxalate, which form when the urine is too acid. It is important to discover which type your cat has as the treatment for each is quite different. FLUTD can be controlled with veterinary prescription diets designed to produce a urine with the correct pH level. The underlying cause of FLUTD is not fully understood, but significant factors include lack of water, too much magnesium in the diet, obesity, lack of exercise and stress. Try to keep your cat slim and active and encourage him to drink plenty of water to flush out the bladder. Avoid over-feeding foods which are high in magnesium, such as pork, beef, heart and oily fish.

Cystitis

Cystitis, or inflammation of the bladder, is usually caused by a bacterial infection. It is also associated with FLUTD (see above) and the symptoms are similar. Cystitis can affect both sexes, but is more common in female cats, particularly tortoiseshells.

Treatment: See a vet as soon as possible. Antibiotic treatment will be needed to remove the bacteria.

CHAPTER
FIVE

Nursing a sick cat

When a cat is ill or recovering from an operation, good nursing care can influence his recovery and prove rewarding for you. What a sick cat needs most is solitude and peace.

■ **Be there for him**, but instruct the children not to fuss over him continually.

■ **Find him a quiet corner** in a warm, airy room and give him clean, snug bedding.

■ **Place his food and water bowls near his bed,** and his litter tray a little way off.

■ **If he is very ill and unable to turn himself over,** gently turn your cat once every two hours to prevent fluid accumulating on the chest.

■ **Ask your vet** about any special nursing or feeding requirements.

■ **Be sure to administer all medications exactly as instructed** by your vet, and always complete the course of treatment, particularly with antibiotics; do not stop as soon as the cat shows signs of improvement.

■ **If your cat refuses to drink he will become dehydrated,** especially if he is vomiting or has diarrhoea. Give him a teaspoon of cool, boiled water, perhaps with a drop of glucose or honey added, every hour or so. Drip it into his mouth slowly, using a dropper inserted at the side of the mouth, letting him swallow after every few drops.

■ **If he refuses to eat, tempt him with warm, nutritious foods,** such as chicken, fish, pilchards, meat- or fish-based baby food, or a liquid invalid food. A light sprinkling of catnip or a catnip-flavoured treat crumbled over food will often encourage a sick cat to eat. If he will not eat from a dish, then feed him from your fingers.

DISPENSING MEDICATION

As most owners know, trying to give a cat medication is a bit like wrestling a hog in mud. Fur flies, teeth and claws flash, the body wriggles or goes into reverse, and a cunning cat will even pretend to swallow the pill and then spit it out when you're not looking. Be firm but gentle and try to remain calm so as not to cause your cat undue distress. Place him on a table, and if he is a struggler get a helper to restrain him while you give the medication, or wrap him securely in a towel.

Giving liquids

Ask your vet for a plastic dropper or syringe.
1 Insert the dropper in the side of the mouth, in the space between the canine and back teeth.
2 Slowly trickle the liquid into the mouth. Give only a few drops at a time and allow the cat to swallow after each dose to avoid choking.

Giving a tablet

Your cat will find a tablet much easier to swallow if you smear it with some butter first.
1 Enclose the cat's head with your fingers and tip it back.
2 Pull down the lower jaw to open the mouth.
3 Drop the pill as far back on the tongue as possible.
4 Quickly close the mouth, keeping the head tilted, and tickle the throat. This will encourage the cat to swallow.

Some cats can be fooled into swallowing a tablet if it is first wrapped in a tasty morsel of chicken, tuna or cream cheese, but do not crush or break a tablet and mix it into the food; cats can detect its odour and will simply refuse to eat. Also, some drugs have a bitter taste which may cause the cat to foam at the mouth.

▌ Administering eye drops

1 Hold the cat's head back and gently drip the drops into the inner corner of the eye. Do not touch the eye with the dropper.
2 Close the eyelids and hold them closed for a few seconds to allow the drops to spread across the eye surface.

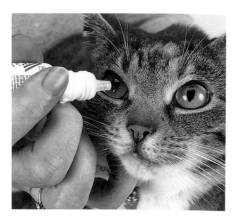

▌ Administering ear drops

1 Turn the cat's head to one side. Fold back the ear flap with one hand and administer the drops with the other.
2 Massage the base of the ear flap to spread the drops well down into the ear canal. When you let go, the cat will shake his head vigorously, so be sure to stand well back!

FIRST AID

Despite your best efforts to keep your beloved pet from harm, accidents will happen, and it's best to be prepared when they do. It is important to remain calm, act swiftly and get your cat to a vet as soon as possible.

Treating a badly injured cat

If you find a cat that has been hit by a car or has had a bad fall, the first priority is to remove him from further danger. This must be done with great care as he may have broken bones and internal injuries. For example, the cat may have a ruptured bladder or a ruptured diaphragm, in which case organs that should be in the abdomen get pushed up into the chest cavity.

Making a 'stretcher'

Use a rug, coat or whatever is to hand to make a 'stretcher' and gently slide the cat on to it, carefully supporting the whole body. Be careful not to twist the body. Hold the head just a little lower than the rest of the body to keep the blood flowing to the brain and keep the cat warm until you reach the veterinary surgery.

Handling an injured cat

If the cat is injured but conscious he will be frightened and in pain and may lash out. Approach him slowly and talk softly so as to reassure him. If possible, wear gloves to protect your hands and avoid putting your face near the cat. Hold him by the scruff of the neck to restrain him while you wrap him in a blanket or towel to prevent him struggling, and keep him warm. Place the cat in a carrier and rush him to the vet. If possible, ask someone to telephone ahead to warn the vet of your arrival.

LIFE-SAVING TECHNIQUES

A badly injured cat may require emergency aid to stop bleeding, treat shock or restart its breathing. Follow the instructions given below, then take the cat to a vet immediately.

▌ Artificial respiration

1 If a cat has stopped breathing but the heart is still beating, remove his collar and lay him on his side with his head tilted downwards to allow blood to flow to the brain.
2 Clear any blood or vomit from the mouth.
3 Pull the tongue forwards to open up the throat. This may stimulate the cat to breathe and he may regain consciousness.
4 If not, press down on the chest with the flat of your hand using a short, sharp push. This expels air from the lungs, allowing them to be refilled with fresh air. Repeat every five seconds until the cat starts to breathe.
5 If there is no sign of life after thirty seconds, try mouth-to-nose respiration: tilt back the cat's head, hold the mouth shut and blow into both nostrils for three seconds to inflate the lungs. Pause for two seconds, then repeat.
6 Continue until the cat starts breathing.
Note: Do not leave an unconscious cat lying on one side for more than 10 minutes; keep turning him, or the lungs may become congested and pneumonia set in.

▌ Controlling bleeding

If an injury is bleeding heavily, firmly apply a cold compress over the wound to stem the blood flow. Do not use disinfectant. If the bleeding does not stop within a few minutes, consult a vet.

Treating shock

When a cat goes into shock there is a lack of blood circulating around his system and he could die. The signs of shock are panting, rapid, shallow breathing and inability to stand. The pupils are enlarged, the ears and paws feel cold and the gums are very pale. The cat needs warmth and fluids. Wrap him in a blanket or, failing that, newspaper, aluminium foil or plastic bubble-wrap, to conserve body heat. Do not apply direct heat, such as a hot-water bottle, as this diverts much-needed blood away from the brain and the internal organs to the skin. Offer a warm drink.

Poisoning

The signs of poisoning depend on the substance involved, but include drooling, severe vomiting and/or diarrhoea, staggering, convulsions and abnormal eye movements.

Contact a vet and tell him what the cat has ingested, if known. There are antidotes to some poisons; for instance, vitamin K injections are the antidote to the commonest form of rat poison, but treatment must be given promptly. Do not induce vomiting unless the vet advises it. If there is paint or oil on the cat's coat, do not use solvents to remove it as these are also very toxic. Soften it with petroleum jelly or vegetable oil, bathe with warm, soapy water and rinse well.

Burns and scalds

If your cat is burned or scalded, flush the burn with lots of cold running water for several minutes. This will give relief and may save the loss of skin. In severe cases, treat for shock and seek veterinary attention. Never apply butter or skin cream to a burn as this only increases the inflammation.

CHAPTER
FIVE

Drowning

After being rescued from the water, a conscious cat should be wrapped in a towel and kept warm.

1 If he is unconscious, hold him, head downwards, by his hind legs and swing him gently back and forth to drain ingested water from his lungs.

2 Lay him on his side with the head lower than the chest. Clear any debris from the mouth and pull the tongue forwards. This should stimulate breathing but, if not, attempt artificial respiration.

Bites and stings

Young cats love to chase insects and often get stung. Remove an embedded bee sting with tweezers or by scraping with a credit card, but don't sqeeze it as it will release more poison. Bee and ant stings are acid so bathe the area with an alkali, such as sodium bicarbonate dissolved in cold water. Wasp stings are alkaline, so treat with an acid antidote such as diluted lemon juice or vinegar. A sting in the mouth or throat may swell rapidly, resulting in asphyxiation, so rush the cat to a vet.

Choking

Choking is less common with cats than with dogs, but a sewing needle or a fish or poultry bone may get lodged against the roof of the mouth or stuck in the throat. A choking cat will panic, so restrain him by wrapping him in a towel. Open the cat's mouth but don't tilt the head back as this may cause the object to drop into the throat. If you can see the object, remove it with blunt-ended tweezers. Do not pull a visible thread as it may be attached to an object in the stomach. If you cannot find the object, seek veterinary help urgently.

Electrocution

Switch off the power and remove the plug from the socket before touching an electrocuted cat, otherwise you too may receive an electric shock. If the cat has chewed through an electrical wire his mouth and tongue may be burned. Electrical burns can result in shock and cardiac arrest. Seek veterinary attention straight away.

Dehydration

Dehydration occurs when a cat loses vital body fluids due to heatstroke, a severe bout of vomiting or diarrhoea, kidney disease or diabetes. Pinch the loose skin at the back of the cat's neck and lift it up. When you release it, it should fall back quickly. If it falls back slowly, the cat is dehydrated. Severe dehydration requires immediate attention as it can cause fits and your cat could die.

Restraining a cat

A mother cat carries her kitten by grasping him in her mouth by the scruff of his neck. A reflex action causes his forequarters to go limp and his hind legs and tail curl up out of the way. This reflex often persists into adulthood, which can come in useful if you need to restrain a cat in an emergency.

1 Grasp him gently but firmly by the scruff of the neck.

2 He will appear to go into a trance and can be lifted, provided his weight is supported by placing your other hand under his hindquarters. Never lift a cat by the scruff without supporting the rump as it can damage the muscles.

FIRST AID